RUDRA SUDHANIDHI

Rudra Sudhanidhi

CELESTIAL JOURNEY OF THE QUINTESSENTIAL SEEKER

NARAYANANANDA ABADHUTA SWAMI

General Editor
UDAYANATH SAHOO

Translated by
BASANT KUMAR TRIPATHY

Introduction by
URMISHREE BEDAMATTA

JNU

ADIKABI SARALA DAS
CHAIR OF ODIA STUDIES
Jawaharlal Nehru University,
New Delhi

MANOHAR
2026

First published 2026
First eBook edition 2026

ISBN 978-93-6080-105-2 (hardbound)
ISBN 978-93-6080-214-1 (eBook)

Published by

Adikabi Sarala Das Chair of Odia Studies,
Jawaharlal Nehru University,
New Delhi 110067
&
Ajay Kumar Jain *for*
Manohar Publishers & Distributors
4753/23 Ansari Road, Daryaganj
New Delhi 110 002

Typeset by Kohli Print, Delhi 110 051

Cover design by Kamal Singh Jammual

Printed and bound in India

This book is the English version of *Rudra Sudhanidhi*, written in Odia by Narayanananda Abadhuta Swami, edited by Krushnacharan Sahoo and published by Friends' Publishers, Binodbehari, Cuttack, 2022, ninth edition.

Contents

Preface

The first-ever prose work in Odia language, *Rudra Sudhanidhi*, written by Narayanananda Abadhuta Swami (early sixteenth century CE) is hailed as a landmark literature as much for its unique theme as for its inimitable style of expression. It mark a shift of the art of story-telling from the oral tradition to a textual tradition at a time when Odia literature was dominated mainly by poetry. It is a gripping account of a young yogi's life which passes through three stages of experience: sin, suffering and the realisation of the ultimate reality. The text also exposes how, in those times, yogis of various sects were in the habit of using their spiritual powers for their personal benefits and creating miracles and magic to prevail on the common people.

Rudra Sudhanidhi is a portrait-gallery of characters belonging to the world of the gods, such as Lord Shiva, Parvati and Lakshmi, of men such as Rudra Sudhanidhi, Abidya, King Dharmadhvaja, Ananga Padmakar, Queen Sashiprava, Kokilabati; of yogis such as Abadhuta and Kamananda; and, of the supernatural such as the ghosts, *betals*, *chandas*, *pretas* and *yoginis* each contributing substantially to the central theme of the story. Divine machinery plays a great part allowing the story to gain speed and suspense.

The story begins with Lord Shiva holding a test of his disciples to know their true qualities—whether they are steadfast in their devotion or not. Upon his request Parvati produces a Mohini Kanya whom he uses as a decoy to enchant the yogis in meditation. Abhinaba Chaitanya, one of the disciples, falls into Kandarpa's trap and loses the test, incurring the displeasure of the Lord. Incensed, the Lord curses him to be born in King Ananga Padmakar's family and experience the pains of human life. He assures him that he would come out as a great yogi if he takes the path of righteousness and will have the opportunity to marry Mohini Kanya in his youth.

In obedience to Lord Shiva's command, he takes shelter in Queen Sashiprava's womb. There, he had a spiritual discourse with an Abadhuta who had come on a visit to the Queen. The discourse develops into an argument in which he defeats Abadhuta. When he was born, a *yogini* named Sutaharini, who used to kill the newly born babies, appeared there to take him away. When her attempts fall through, she surrenders to him and takes his advice to become a devotee of Lord Vasudeva. The newly born child is named *Rudra Sudhanidhi*. As he grows up, he learns all the shastras he lays his hands on. The king sends his men in all four directions to find a suitable bride for him. The messengers return empty-handed, informing the king that nowhere could they find a suitable match.

Meanwhile Goddess Lakshmi happens to meet Abidya on the bank of the Manasarovara. Impressed by her beauty and manners, she thought of offered her to Queen Kokilabati, wife of King Dharmadhvaja, who had been praying to her for a child since long. When the time to search for a bridegroom for her approached, her maids showed her the portraits of many young men, of which she selected the portrait of *Rudra Sudhanidhi*. But before the wedding, Kamananda yogi, a Tantrik, appears on the scene and prevails upon *Rudra Sudhanidhi* after his attempts to abdut Cbidya fail miserably. The story ends abruptly while a pair of singers continues singing, glorifying the charms and manners of princess Abidya.

By bringing the Abadhuta, Sutaharini and Kamananda, the author intends to present three sets of yogis who are fake because they lack devotion to Vasudeva, the only one to grant salvation. *Rudra Sudhanidhi* could overcome all of them because of his unflinching devotion to Lord Vasudeva. The author emphasizes Vaishnavism and believes it to be superior to Shaivism or the

Shakta tradition. It leads a devotee to stay away from the bitter flavour of mortal rivalry and helps him vindicate God's ways to man.

The Language of the text is unique—a mix of the lyrical and the intellectual, as if poetry is pushing itself forward to mingle into prose. The words in the lyrical part of the sentence rhyme, while the other part is written in either colloquial or sophisticated language. This harmonious blending of prose and poetry symbolizes the transitional period in which poetry ends and prose begins.

Considering the concept and the linguistic pattern, it can be concluded that *Rudra Sudhanidhi* is a unique creation that reflects not only the elements of literature but also the history and traditions that surround it. While explaining elaborately the tricks of yoga throughout the text; the author sends a message to the society to distinguish between the fakes and the genuine and how to maintain the purity of mind in a world of earthly temptations.

SANTISHREE DHULIPUDI PANDIT
Vice-Chancellor
Jawaharlal Nehru University

Foreword

Adikabi Sarala Das Chair of Odia Studies started its activities at the Jawaharlal Nehru University (JNU) with the financial help of the Government of Odisha on 26 December 2017 in the Centre of Indian Languages (CIL), School of Language, Literature and Culture Studies (SLL & CS). The Chair intends to represent Odisha, its language, literature and culture in all its multilingual and pluralistic manifestations. The Chair encourages comparative studies across a wide range of the domains and also aims at disseminating knowledge of Odia language, literature and culture, both at the national and international levels.

As a realistic approach to meet the objectives the Chair has launched a number of projects, one of which is translating ancient and medieval Odia classics into Indian and foreign languages. The English version of *Bichitra Ramayana,* a fifteenth-century epic, was published in 2020 and another epic *Chandi Purana,* written by Adikabi Sarala Das, was translated into English and published in 2022. The same year the Hindi version of *Pranaya Ballari*, one of the most popular Odia epics, written by Gangadhar Meher was published. This year we are bringing out the English rendering of the first-ever prose work in Odia language, *Rudra Sudhanidhi,* composed by Narayanananda Abadhuta Swami, which marks the beginning of the Age of Odia Katha literature.

Written somewhere between 1506 and 1526, the story is divided into five parts demonstrating the fall and rise of a Shaivite *yogi,* the metamorphosis of Abhinaba Chaitanya into *Rudra Sudhanidhi.* Part 1 describes how he fell out of Lord Shiva's favour when he failed to stifle his emotion at the sight of Mohini Kanya whom the Lord used as a decoy to test the true qualities of his disciples. For his failure in maintaining the moral standards of a *yogi*, the Lord cursed him to be born again on the earth and experience the sorrows and sufferings of human life. No matter how long or how benignly he prayed to him to take back the curse, the Lord was unmoved. He, however, consoled him by giving details of what his next life was going to be like. He said that he would be born as the son of Ananga Padmakar, the king of Basudha Mandala. His wife Sashiprava, had been praying for a son since long and Abhinaba Chaitanya would fulfil her long cherished dream.

In Part 2, the scene shifts from the Jitashram cave of the Kailas to Basudha Mandala kingdom as Abhinaba Chaitanya, through Tarak Dhatu *yoga*, transferred his life to a lump of sperm and entered Queen Sashiprava's womb and settled there. With each passing day he felt the painful changes related to the birth process, but tried his best to clutch to the memories of his past life and his devotion to Vasudeva. There came a day when an *abadhuta* reached the king's palace. He was a discontented soul and of boastful nature. Following the path of *tantra*, he had attained *siddhi*, but it did not give him peace or spiritual joy. He considered the world to be a pollen grain and regarded Brahma, Vishnu and Mahesvar as insects. When asked about the child in the womb, he sat in meditation, reduced himself to a molecule and spoke to the child from the queen's earlobe. The long conversion that went on between them enlightened him with the true knowledge of God; he realized that devotion to Vasudeva and renouncement of all worldly things is the only path to spiritual happiness. Accepting the child as his *guru*, he left.

Part 3 describes the birth of the child later named as Rudra Sudhanidhi. Whereas other babies used to cry 'Kuhu Kuhu' this one, at the moment of his birth, cried out 'Shivoham'. Just then a *yogini* called Sutaka Harini arrived there to take his life. Aware of her intention, Rudra sat in *meru-mudra* which made his body stick to the ground firmly. In spite of repeated attempts to carry him away, Sutaka Harini failed to do so. Seeing this, the baby burst into laughter that surprised her. He spoke to her on how she was wasting her life in taking recourse to despicable crimes and gave her a set of advice for improvement. His words made her realize her mistakes and she expressed her eagerness to abide by what he would ask her to do. Rudra advised her to chant the name of Vasudeva and work as his nurse till he grew up. She shed off her terrible appearance, changed into a beautiful woman and looked after him since then. Towards the end of the chapter, we see Rudra Sudhanidhi as a young man, well-versed in all *shastras* and equipped with the knowledge of warfare. It was time for the king to look for a bride for him. The messengers, sent in four directions to find a bride came back empty-handed with no positive information. The king worried himself sick about his son's marriage.

Part 4 is dominated by one Kamananda Yogi, a great *tantrik*, who had command and authority over ghosts, *betalas*, *yakshinis*, *chandas*, *daityas* and *yoginis*. Pleased with his devotion, Goddess Bhubaneswari wished to offer him a boon. She told him that the best thing a *yogi* could wish for was salvation which could only be granted by Vasudeva. Kamananda wilfully rejected the proposal. He explained that he wished for a life of sensual pleasure, not the liberation of his soul. He considered the pleasures of the flesh to be true happiness and begged her for it. She cautioned him against the dangers accompanyimg such a life, but when he declined to take her advice, she granted him the boon he was asking for. She taught him a specific yogic exercise that would fulfil his wish, which included washing bowels, *asana*, *pranayama*, *pranab*, dieting, meditation, *dharana* and *samadhi*. Following her instructions, he attained *siddhi* and acquired enormous yogic powers.

The last part of the story is packed with fast-moving actions that set in motion a series of important events, central to the theme of the story. Informed about Abidya Mrutyusanjibani Karani by Anila Khechara, his minister, Kamananda Yogi was erotically stimulated. The minister filled him in on the details of the history of her life—how Parvati produced her from her body and asked her to sit in meditation on the banks of the Manasarovara, how Lakshmi saw her and declared her as her daughter and how, finally, she came to be the daughter of King Dharmadhvaja and Queen Kokilabati of Prithi Tilak Kingdom. He mentioned categorically that she was destined to marry Rudra Sudhanidhi only. The way he narrated her beauty and virtues excited Kamananda's senses who vowed to have her, no matter how difficult it might be. He employed all his means to abduct her; he even sent Chandi for the purpose, but all his attempts were in vain as Dharmadhvaja's kingdom was guarded by Vishnu's *sudarsana* wheel. Having no other alternative, he decided to make friends with Rudra Sudhanidhi and kidnap Abidya after they marry each other. He displayed many miracles to prevail on him. Being informed of his spiritual powers, King Ananga Padmakar invited him to his palace. While a conversation was going on between them two singers, Madhu and Malati reached there. Their song glorified Abidya's beauty and before they could end their song, the story came to an end abruptly.

Rudra Sudhanidhi is a gripping narrative of the world of mystics, where the pursuit of enlightenment, austerity, renouncement and progress towards divinity are prioritized. It deals with the religious conflict that arose among various sects of Hindu religion in sixteenth-century Odisha, creating an atmosphere of falsehood and immorality. The primary objective of the author is to bring unity among the cults such as the Shaivism, the Shakta and the Vaishnavism to establish the supremacy of Vaishnavism over the other two. Besides, he attempts to show that Shiva, Vishnu and Bhubanesvari are one and the same; they all belong to the larger tradition of Hindu spiritualism. Written in a lyrical and rhythmical poetic pattern, *Rudra Sudhanidhi* is a classic in Odia literature.

On this occasion I express my sincere thanks to Professor Basant Kumar Tripathy for undertaking the translation of this landmark volume into English and to Dr. Urmishree Bedamatta for providing us with a brilliant piece of Introduction with relevant references. I am also thankful to Ajay Kumar Jain of Manohar Publishers and Distributors, New Delhi, for taking the onerous task of publishing this classical text jointly with Adikabi Sarala Das Chair of Odia studies at CIL/SLL&CS, Jawaharlal Nehru University. Last but not least I express my heart-felt gratitude to Madam Vice-Chancellor for her cooperation and contast encouragement in making the project a success.

PROF. UDAYANATH SAHOO
Chair Professor
Adikabi Sarala Das Chair of Odia Studies
CIL/SLL & CS, Jawaharlal Nehru University

Introduction
The Journey of a *Siddha*

I

Rudra Sudhanidhi[1] is set in the mystical realm of Jitashram in mount Kapilas,[2] which is inhabited by none other than the Lord of lords, Shiva, and his consort Parvati, Lakshmi and her consort

[1] The editor of the Odia palm leaf manuscript of *Rudra Sudhanidhi*, Karunakar Kar, citing linguistic and verse forms, dates the composition to the first half of the sixteenth century. This makes the text part of, as David G. White says, 'the siddha legacy in modern India', and may have been a popular hagiography of a siddha who once resided in the Kapilas mountain in the Odisha region. White's observation on the life and practice of medival siddhas offers a context for *Rudra Sudhanidhi:* 'The medieval Siddhas of India were self-styled imitators of divine and semidivine Siddhas who, through their conjoined practice of alchemy, haṭha yoga, and tantric ritual (erotio-mystical or 'sublimated', when it took the form of worship of the divine Siddhas), sought to join the ranks of the latter at the end of their practice (*sadhana*) or at the end of their lives. Over the centuries, the cults of the divine Siddhas and Vidyādharas, denizens of the atmospheric region or of lofty peaks, have gradually diminished and are today found only in remote mountain regions of the Indian sub-continent. In other parts of India, these demigods have been supplanted by or conflated with such historical figures as Matsyendrnāth, Gorakhnāth, Nāgārjuna, or Dattātreya, figures who self-consciously aligned themselves with the former, taking their names as honorary titles or indications of various degrees of realization in their mystic arts (p. 335).'

[2] Kapilas or 'Kapilasa' is also a famous mountain located in the

Vishnu, Kamadeva, who is always seen lurking on the fringes, the *avadhutas* and the *rudras* or *siddhas*.[3] The *siddhas* are portrayed as being proud of their achievements and have taken refuge at Vishnu's feet, practising austerity and *yoga* to purify their hearts and minds. They have downplayed the cosmic *lila* (divine play) of God as mere magic, and they seem to have a different interpretation of feminine grace and the allure of women. Shiva and Parvati, as part of their divine sport, wish to test the determination of a special *rudra siddha* called Abhinaba Chaitanya. Abhinaba Chaitanya had been making great strides in the world of spirituality and was prideful as he was beginning to acquire the status of a god when Shiva and his wife

---

Dhenkanal district of Odisha. A multitude of devotees throngs the renowned abode of Shiva on the night of Shivaratri, when the Nath Yogis are believed to stand vigil over the temple. The name 'Kapilas' not only evokes the image of 'Kailas' but also suggests that the narrative may have its roots in the renunciate tradition. This connection is significant, especially considering that Kailas despite being perceived as a sacred pilgrimage site in later interpretations, was historically viewed as a mataphorical idea rather than a real destination accessible to ordinary pilgrims. See McKay for a compelling exposition on renunciants and their practices, highlighting their unique spiritual journeys and the profound impact of their traditions on broader cultural and philosophical landscapes.

[3] In the Indian tradition, Siddha is used as a genric term for someone who has achieved mastery or spritual accomplishment, often through esoteric practices or mystical formulas. Bharti explains that the term 'Siddha' encompasses individuals in both the Shaiva and Buddhist traditions. However, in regional literatures, the worshippers of Shiva are typically referred to as 'nath yogis', those in the Buddhist tantric tradition are known as 'siddhas' (see Bharti, p. 19)

decided to call upon Kamadeva, also known as Manmath or Makaradhvaja.

Makaradhvaja has a strong grudge against the *siddhas*, considering them his arch enemies. He vows to cut them into pieces and burn them with the help of the Mohini Kanya's sidelong glances. He is confident in his ability to wipe out the *siddhas*, who had previously considered themselves unconquerable. The *rudra siddhas*, who had previously thought they had beaten him, are bewildered by the impact of his presence. When Mohini Kanya appears, the fierce control of the *siddhas* is torn asunder:

It was as if Manmath flew wasps among a quiet flock of birds or a deluge of the maiden's beauty submerged the mountains of the fortitude of the *yogis* or ignorance overshadowed wisdom or a cloud of unintelligence covered the rising moon of their intellect or the advent of spring endangered the peaceful lives of the lotuses in bloom or the enchanting appearance of the woman disturbed their quest for enlightenment or a stream of nectar flowing from her lips put out the fire of the yogic practices.

Even Abhinaba Chaitanya fell prey to Mohini Kanya's beauty:

His senses excited, he was afloat on the waves of lust.

Shiva! Shiva! The air in the *sushumna nadi*, instead of flowing upwards, moved downwards. The unfettered elephant fell into the bog of enchantment. Hari! Hari! He broke with the tradition that he abided by so far.

[. . .]

Poor Rudra! Struck by Kandarpa's five arrows, he was drowned in the sea of sorrow. He had gambled away all his wisdom and fallen prey to Kandarpa's wrath. He had taken leave of his senses by submitting himself to the earthly pleasures. His demure face was speckled with beads of sweat. His lips shook like wisps of hair flopping over the forehead when a mild wind blew. He yawned and tittered. He shook in horror, his eyes set down.

Shiva chastizes Abhinaba:

You reaped as you had sown. You will have this woman as your wife only when you are born again. Listen! A *yogi*, after his downfall, becomes either a Sambhulinga whom no one worships or a king. Now be prepared to undergo all kinds of sufferings. Go and take shelter in the womb of Sashiprava, the chief queen of Ananga Padmakar.

Abhinaba Chaitanya cries out in despair. Singing his glory, he beseeches upon the Lord to have mercy on him, and the Lord responds thus:

My son, Abhinaba Chaitanya! Why do you fret so much? Can misfortune befall someone as learned as you are? Nevertheless how can one get away with doing something wrong? Birth and death are indispensable for every living being and you are no exception. Your *karma*, prompted by your earthly desires, ended up in wrong-doing. Consequent upon the sin you committed, you are liable to suffer the agony of birth and death. This is how you will have to pay for your sin, which the Vedas call *prarabdha*. Now you will be born again and lead your life as luxuriously as Lord Indra does. In the long run you will receive God's blessings.

In the history of yogic adventure, *Rudra Sudhanidhi* is, a dramatic tale of rivalry, power, and determination among divine beings, and Abhinaba Chaitanya emerges as the quintessential seeker, a determined Siddha venturing on an odyssey of self-discovery and spiritual enlightenment. Like a mesmerizing tale woven by the cosmos itself, this journey unfolds with the human soul caught in the labyrinth of a self-imposed curse, ensnared by the very desires that promised ephemeral joys and pleasures.

This sacred voyage is not for the faint of heart, but rather for the brave souls who dare to venture beyond the boundaries of ordinary existence. The seeker, with an unwavering determination, faces the tempest of desires with the serenity of a sage, transmuting the trials into stepping stones on the path to liberation.

In this exploration, salvation is not achieved through the suppression of desire but rather through its mastery. The Siddha embraces the challenges presented by a morally flawed world, viewing them as opportunities for growth. Bharti, in the begining of his book, *Siddha Sahitya*, references a verse from Siddha Tilopa, who likens the process of detachment to the gradual immunity developed by an individual who consistently ingests poison. Just as such a person becomes resistant to the poison's effects over time, so too does one who fully engages with worldly pleasures gradually transcend attachment to them.[4]

Thus, in the yogic tradition, the seeker's journey unfolds amid a treacherous dance of desires, which ultimately leads to the liberation of the soul. As they traverse the labyrinth of existence in the earthly realm, Basudha Mandala, they, which includes *avadhutas* and *siddha yogis*, discover the alchemy of heaven, transforming the mundane into the divine and unearthing the infinite potential within their very being. This celestial pilgrimage of the seeker serves as an eternal reminder that salvation lies within, waiting to be awakened and embraced with open arms.

II

In the ancient world of yore, *yoga* transcended mere physical exercise; it was a tortuous way of life, a journey that led seekers

[4] जिम विस भक्खइ विसहिं पलुत्ता / तिम भव भुंजइ भवहिं ए जुत्ता। (जैसे विश्र के (निरन्तर) भक्षण करने से (मनुष्य) विष के प्रभाव से मुक्त हो जाता है, वैसे ही भव का भोग करने से फिर भव में लिप्त नहीं होता)

(or, jim vis bhakhai visahin palutta/tim bhav bhunjai bhavhin e jutta) to channel their life-force, seeking a state of serene detachment from worldly desires. Those who successfully attained such a transcendent state were known as *siddhas*, revered beings of wisdom and enlightenment. As time passed and the rigours of ascetic practices grew more challenging, the number of aspiring *siddhas* likely dwindled. However, the steadfast souls who remained on this noble path continued their relentless pursuit, undeterred by the hardships that lay ahead.

In this hallowed discipline of *yoga*, as in any revered art, the need arose to guide and train new aspirants. Thus, a rich textual canon was diligently constructed, serving as a roadmap to illumination for those embarking on the yogic quest. Countless sacred texts were penned, each containing invaluable wisdom and profound insights into the divine mysteries.

Among these tales, the captivating story of *Rudra Sudhanidhi* once known as Abhinaba Chaitanya stands as a testament to the transformative power of yogic or disciplined life. The path that Abhinaba embarked upon demanded a deep understanding of the sacred scriptures and a profound dedication to inner growth. It was through the teachings of these revered texts that Abhinaba was initiated into the mystical yogic way of life.

Rudra Sudhanidhi is a biography which unfolds the extraordinary journey of a seeker, a sacred homage to the life of an enlightened soul who walked this path before. Within its pages, the essence of divine grace and perseverance intertwine, painting a vivid story of spiritual devotion and unwavering determination. In the world of yesteryears, where yogic wisdom flowed like a sacred river, the pursuit of enlightenment was not merely an ambition but a way of being. Those who treaded this illustrious path were the torch bearers of ancient wisdom, preserving the sacred teachings for generations to come. And so, the legacy of *yoga*, steeped in ancient traditions, continues to inspire souls across the ages, inviting them to embark on the sacred journey of self-discovery and transformation. *Rudra Sudhanidhi*, echoes the story of every fallen soul, entangled in the seductive web of earthly desires, only to yearn for redemption and seek the path of non-attachment once more.

At the heart of this narrative lies a soul, once radiant and pure, basking in the celestial light of divine consciousness. Yet, amidst the allure of the material realm, the soul succumbs to the allure of worldly temptations. Driven by the primal cravings of the flesh, it veers off the path of spiritual clarity and finds itself immersed in the transient pleasures of the physical realm. In this pursuit of fleeting gratification, the soul momentarily forgets its true nature, believing in the illusion that material possessions and sensory pleasures will satiate the inner void. Alas, the more it grasps at the transient, the emptier it feels, as if its very essence is slipping through its fingers like grains of sand. Yet, amidst the darkness of its own making, a flicker of inner wisdom remains, a sacred ember waiting to be reignited. It is in the depths of this despair that the soul awakens to the realization that true fulfilment lies not in the external world but in the boundless realm within. And, therefore,

Carrying out the Lord's command, Abhinaba Chaitanya bowed to Goddess Parvati and sat in lotus posture. Of the sixty-four types of *yoga*, he chose the one called Taraka Dhatu Yoga. He united the *nadi*s such as *inla*, *pingala*, *sushumna*, *alambusa*, *kaukshani*, *gandhari*, *hastijihva* and *sankhini* with many other *nadi*s such as *naga*, *kurma*, *krukalaka*, *debadatta*, *dhananjay*, *apana*, *byana*, *samana* and *udana*. He, then, directed the energy called *kundalini* to the lotus at his heart, in the shape of *Om*.

Abhinaba's exercise is a standard practice of directing human consciousness inward and has been elaborated with finer details in the traditional yogic canon such as the *Nirvana Upanishad*, which scholars have classed under a group of minor Upanishads called *Upanishads of Renunciation* or *Samnyasa Upanishads*[5] the *Bhavan Upanishad*,[6] and others.[7]

As it ascends the arduous path of self-mastery, the soul learns to cultivate non-attachment, not in denial of the world, but in a state of harmonious detachment. It understands that true freedom is not the absence of desires, but the transcendence of their binding grip. The soul now dances to a different rhythm, guided by the melodic whispers of the universe. Its actions are no longer driven by insatiable cravings but inspired by compassion, love, and service to all beings. It finds solace in the present moment, embracing the beauty of impermanence, and cherishing the eternal nature of the soul's essence.

Through the trials and tribulations of its soul's journey, *Rudra Sudhanidhi* emerges as a profound allegory, a mirror reflecting the delicate interplay of human existence. It reminds us that we are all susceptible to the allure of desires, and yet,

[5] Cited in Patrick Olivelle, *Samnyasa Upanisads*, p. 5. The Samnyasa [Sanyasa] Upanishads, which were translated and critically edited by German scholars, Paul Deussen and F. Otto Schrader respectively, include seven to twenty minor Upanishads. However, the Sanyasa Upanishads do not represent a traditional classification of the Upanishads in India. Paul Deussen was the first to use this category to describe these texts 'according to the tendency predominant in them' (ibid.). According to Olivelle, these Upanishads are significant not only for understanding the history of Indian ascetical institutions but also for tracing the development of Brahmanical theology related to renunciation (p. 5).

[6] *Bhaavanoopanishat* (for a scholarly edition of *Bhavan Upanishad* in Sanskrit, see *Saundarya Lahari with Lakshmidhara Commentary, Bhavana Upanishad with Bhaskar Commentary* and *Devi Pancha Stavi*) cited in *The Technology of Lambika Yoga.*

[7] Other similar texts cited in *The Technology* are, *Maanasollaasa* and *Hathayoga Pradeepika.*

within each of us lies the potential for redemption and spiritual reawakening. And so, the tale of Abhinaba Chaitanya beckons us to tread mindfully on our own paths, to recognize the ever-present invitation to return to the state of non-attachment, and to embrace the profound wisdom that awaits those who embark on the journey of rediscovering their true selves.

III

In the enigmatic world of ancient wisdom, emerges Kamananda, a *siddha* contra valere. Like Abhinaba, he is a seeker but is attended upon by sixty-four *yoginis* who assist him as he gets ensnared in the tantalizing allure of worldly power and pleasure.[8]

Reciting the one-lettered *mantra* and offering animal sacrifices, he had pleased Bhubanesvari who commanded the six *chakras* and her followers such as Lakeni, Kakeni, Hakini, Dakini and Bakini. Adorned with a crown of crescent moon, she appeared before him and said, 'Kamananda! I will fulfil your wishes'. Lying prostrate before her, the *yogi* begged her with folded hands, 'Your kind words make me feel like I am drinking nectar'. When the Goddess told him to ask for a boon, he replied, 'Grant me what you consider the best for a human'. The Goddess explained, 'The best thing for

[8] Kamananda's character seems to echo in those who believe in the Tantra dictum *Bhogo Yogayathe*. Sri M., in *The Journey Continues*, explains the dictum as 'Yoga or union with the Divine through *Bhoga* (enjoyment or indulgence). It is because of this that many conclude that Tantra is the practice of midnight drunken orgies, where sex is freely indulged in' (p. 85). Siddha literature offers a profound explanation of *Bhogo Yogayathe*: *jis vis bhakkhai visahin palutta/tim bhava bhunjai bhavahin na jutta* (trans. 'Just as repeated exposure to poison builds immunity, indulging in worldly pleasures repeatedly fosters detachment from the world'.), Siddha Tilopa cited in Dharmavir Bharti, *Siddha Sahitya.*

a man is to aspire for salvation which is not within my jurisdiction. None other than Srikrishna can grant it. I would advise you to try for it.' 'What is salvation?' the *yogi* asked. The Goddess replied, 'It is that state of mind in which there is no contact, no action, no intellect, no ego, no consciousness, no dreaming-only the being, a condition of deep joyful experience, beyond consciousness. It is the symbol of Truth, Eternity and Immortality. It is the Ultimate Reality that exists for all eternity.' The *yogi* asked, 'Is there any room for worldly enjoyment in salvation? Can one have delicious food to eat? Can one make love to beautiful women? Can one possess divine powers? Can he have things that are rare?'

His journey, while extraordinary, unfolds as a poignant reminder of the human struggle to transcend the shackles of desires.

Endowed with profound yogic abilities, Kamananda treads a path where his mastery over the subtle energies of the body allows him to wield extraordinary control. However, amidst the intoxicating elixir of power and the seductive dance of desires, he finds himself entangled in a web of illusion. The crux of Kamananda's tribulation lies in his pursuit of pleasure, seeking transient gratification from the material realm. The downward flow of his semen, a symbol of primal energy, serves as a powerful metaphor for his downward spiral into the realm of desires. In traditional yogic practice, the aspiration is to direct this vital energy upward, channelling it towards spiritual transformation and self-realization. Yet, for Kamananda, the purity of this essence is tainted by its misdirection, embodying the futility of his quest for satisfaction in external pleasures. Powered by the evil ministrations of his assistant Anila Khechara, Kamananda devotes himself fully to his own immersion in the darkness of ignorance, by coveting the tantalizingly beautiful Abidya Mrutyusanjibani Karani who is destined to be taken as wife by Abhinaba Chaitanya.

Although the original manuscript abruptly ends with a song glorifying the beauty of Abidya, it is not difficult to imagine that Kamananda would soon come to grapple with the realization that true fulfilment eludes him in the realm of fleeting desires. The pursuit of worldly power and pleasure may yield temporary highs, but it would leave his soul yearning for something deeper and more meaningful.

In the mystical domain of *Rudra Sudhanidhi*, a panorama of diverse spiritual aspirants unfolds, each possessing their own unique virtues and flaws. Diligent and sincere seekers walk alongside deceptive and malevolent characters. Souls and power-hungry individuals traverse this intricate yogic world. In this labyrinthine journey, the path of *yoga* proves to be as enigmatic as the external world, filled with unexpected twists and turns. The gods themselves, in their divine wisdom, employ cunning decoys to test the unwavering determination of aspiring *yogis*. They employ every means possible to lead them astray, challenging their resolve and commitment to the sacred path.

For the seekers, the trials and tribulations on this spiritual odyssey are formidable. Even the slightest misstep or momentary lapse in focus can lead them to veer off the path of righteousness. Once strayed, the road to reclaiming the path becomes arduous and demanding, as they must navigate through the shadows of self-doubt and confusion.

The true essence of *Rudra Sudhanidhi* lies not merely in the destination but in the drama of the journey itself. Every step taken and every decision made, under the watchful eyes of gods and deities, adds layers of complexity to the seeker's quest. It is through these trials that the aspirants learn the invaluable lessons of resilience, fortitude, and self-discovery.

Within the complex narrative of *Rudra Sudhanidhi*, the grave ills and dangers that lurk along the path of a *yogi* aspiring to become a *siddha* are dramatically portrayed. The journey is strewn with temptations, illusions, and adversities, and it is in facing these challenges that the true mettle of a seeker is tested.

Through the trials and tribulations of Abhinaba Chaitanya, *Rudra Sudhanidhi* serves as a compelling reflection of the human condition, mirroring the universal struggles we all face in our quest for higher truths. The story of Abhinaba resonates as a powerful reminder that the path of a seeker is not one of ease and comfort but a daring adventure, filled with both peril and promise. It illuminates the path of transformation, where seekers must confront their innermost desires, vanquish their inner demons, and rise above the allure of the material world. It is in this dramatic presentation of the human soul's journey that the seeds of wisdom and inspiration take root, guiding aspiring souls towards the sacred goal of becoming a *siddha*, an enlightened being bathed in the eternal light of divine consciousness.

REFERENCES

Bharti, Dharmavir, *Siddha Sahitya.* Prayag, Kitab Mahal, 1955.

Kar, Karunakar, ed., *Rudra Sudhanidhi by Narayanananda Abadhuta Swami.* Bhubaneswar: Orissa Sahitya Akademi, 1965.

McKay, Alex, *Kailas Histories: Renunciate Traditions and the Construction of Himalayan Sacred Geography.* Leiden, Boston: Brill, 2015.

Olivelle, Patrick, tr. & ed., *The Samnyasa Upanisads: Hindu Scriptures on Asceticism and Renunciation.* New York: Oxford University Press, 1992.

Sri M., *The Journey Continues: A Sequel to Apprenticed to a Himalayan Master.* Bangalore: Magenta Press, 2017.

Saundarya Lahari with Lakshmidhara Commentary Bhavana Upanishad with Bhaskar Commentary and Devi Pancha Stavi, Mysore Oriental Research Institute Series 114, Jangamwadi Math Collection. Mysore: Prachya Vidya Samshodhanalaya, Mysore University, 1953.

White, David Gordon, *The Alchemical Body: Siddha Traditions in Medieval India.* Chicago: University of Chicago Press, 1996.

Yogiraja Vaidyaraja, *The Technology of Lambika Yoga: Khechari Siddhi.* Alamuru, East Godavary: Rajayogasadhanashram.

URMISHREE BEDAMATTA

CHAPTER 1

Abhinaba Chaitanya Fails the Test

I bow to Hari and Hara.

Sheltered in Sri Ekamra grove, I am Sri Bhubanesvari's darling son, sinless, an eloquent speaker, of divine origin, a human incarnation of Sarada, the greatest of all distinguished learned men, the Purest of the pure in heart and mind, the greatest *pundit* in his youth, a miniature version of Panchanana, a lion in human form, well-versed in the Vedas, six scriptures, nine books of grammar, eighteen Puranas, the *Gita*, thirty-six scriptures of Smruti tradition, plays, *tantrika* practices including *stambhana, mohana, basya, ucchatana, repana, rasa, rasayana*, *ulluka, kuhuka, mani* and *mantramahausadhi.*

Thus says Narayanananda Abadhuta.

In dispelling the dark secrets of *Brahman*, I am a lamp encrusted with nine gems. I can stop the movement of the universe at will. Some will believe it, others will express their doubts. So I will refer to the times when creation was taking root and say something. Say what? That which Hara told Parvati in the Kailas.

It was past sunset; the hills along the shore of the Manasarovara were flooded with moonlight. There, in the Jitashram cave of the beautiful Kailas, a part of the Meru Mountain, located in Bharata, the Destroyer of Kamadeva and the daughter of Mountain king were present with their followers called *siddharudras* in an academic atmosphere. Which simile can best describe the scene? Through our deep meditation he appeared to us as lovely as the full moon, placed beside the beautiful Rohini, surrounded by the stars, above the white clouds of autumn, bypassing the malevolent planets. He was a *mahatma* no doubt, but how did the *siddharudra*s look like? Pure in heart and mind and absolutely in quest of the Ultimate Reality, they were sitting in lotus posture with unblinking eyes, supremely indifferent to earthly pleasures, eager to listen to the voice of the other world, having achieved command over their senses. Sitting still in meditation in pursuit of enlightenment, they were free from the mundane world, and, as their heart was pure and conscience clear, they had kept the passions such as impatience, fear and anxiety at bay. Thinking at Narayan's feet, they were committed to vindicate the ways of God, the Supreme Soul and sat around Trilochan like a girdle. As instructed by the Lord, they considered the body to be as loathsome as clothes to a drunken man.

Watching them with compassionate eyes, the Lord of lords thought of taking a test of their true qualities. With this in mind, the Lord of the universe called Parvati and whispered to her in a sweet voice: 'O dear, the most benevolent and enlightened one! You manifest in everything from grass to *Brahman* in form of *maya* which underlies every creation. Are these *yogi*s on the right path or not? I wish to know their virtues and vices. Dear mine! I would like to ask you to produce a Mohini Kanya to seduce the *siddharudra*s. Kandarpa takes shelter in your hips. Don't have any apprehensions. You'll produce her from your soul. That Kamadeva will accompany the Mohini Kanya, armed with his bow of flowers. We'll get our work done by him. Let's see the extent of power he enjoys.'

At his command, Kamadeva, God who rules the mind, sprang into action. To prevail on those who had renounced the world, Parvati gave birth to a beautiful maiden from her mind after a moment of meditation.

Lo! That maiden enchanted the whole world, causing a flutter in every heart. It seemed as if the sea of Ananga had surged into the cave of the Kailas. What a miraculous impact it had on the earth! Was it an illusion created by Manmath's bow? Was she a glorious flash of lightning or a trap to capture Brahma and other gods or a sprawl of beauty designed by the creator or an urn filled with the nectar of love or an angle-rod to lure the fish of the minds of the *yogis* or Goddess Lakshmi herself or the consort of Kandarpa or a night filled with celestial light or a fierce storm powerful enough to put out the lamp of conscience or a sweet smile to enchant God or to excite Kandarpa's senses? Her face shone like the full moon in the autumn sky. Her eyes were like a snare to trap the *yogis*. They were like the tide of River Ganga determined to uproot the tree of knowledge. Her sly glances could force a *yogi* forsake his wish for *nirvana*. A look at her face would send Lord Shiva to a state of trance and the creator to fits of delirium. Seeing her, the moon felt restless; he developed a sense of dislike for Rohini. Failing to stand her sight, the moon's face turned pale and dark, which people viewed as black spots. She was born with the sole purpose of beguiling the minds of those who boasted of their victory over senses. Brihaspati, when he saw her, would simmer in the heat of love. If Indra's eyes fell on her breasts which were like the fruits of Kalpabata, he would prefer serving at her feet to relishing the beauty of heaven. It seemed as if those, who were in habit of despizing women, had disappeared from the world with her arrival.

Out of fun Lakshmi shut Narayan's lotus-eyes with both of her hands. It was as if the maiden was the eternal source of feminine beauty. All divine wonders seemed much inferior to the spell she cast on all men. After all she was the darling child of the Mother of the Universe! Leaving his fascination for women aside, Kandarpa had been sheltering in her hips and carrying out her orders. The sight of her thighs would induce Kubera to forfeit all his wealth. The sun, bewitched by her beauty, would descend on the earth, leaving Chhaya behind. She filled the river of amusement with waters of her beauty. The age of glorifying the so-called glamorous women of the three worlds had come to an end. Her beauty stunned the *dikpalas*.The living beings as well as the non-living felt a new lease of life. It seemed as if she was the urn of nectar which Lakshmi had brought from the sea while it was being churned. As instructed by the Goddess of the Universe, she swirled the *yogis*' sea of knowledge. In her attempt to lure them into Kamadeva's snare, she reached the assembly of the *mahatmas* who were in a state of *samadhi*. Decked in finery, she was all set to distract their attention from *yoga* by her sidelong glances. Kandarpa, armed with five arrows, stood by her. Soon spring arrived there, later to be joined by the moon which shone in the clear sky.

The evening thickened into night. A light wind blew with a calming touch. It filled the youth with a fiery passion. Bitten by Kandarpa, the wild beasts felt extremely restless. The *vidyadharis* roaming there were erotically stimulated. Green leaves appeared on withered trees. The unwilling cow-elephants had to bear with the sexual harassment by the male ones far bigger than themselves. Some of the wind sneaked into the clothes covering the breasts of the damsels of heaven, only to be embarrassed. The cuckoos sang and parrots talked off-season. Bumble bees blushed to kiss the lotuses, their bodies upturned. The beasts of the forest went wild. Men preferred to take shelter in the arms of their women.

Finding the *rudras* completely bewildered by the impact of his presence, Manmath put the five arrows on his bow, and, taking the aim, sternly said:

Let me see today how the boastful *siddhas* will escape from my hands. They had been under the impression that they had beaten me. They are proud of their wonderful achievement. With austerity, they took refuge at Vishnu's feet and purified their hearts and minds. Through *yoga* they have learnt how to hear the voice of conscience and abide by it. They downplayed God's cosmic lila as an act of magic. They equated the eternal feminine grace with hell. They interpreted the seductive looks of women as mere distraction. Because of the immunity of these stupid fellows to worldly temptations, we, the six brothers, had to flee this place. They are my arch enemies; let me see who comes to their rescue today.

Wrapped in such thoughts, Makaradhvaja traced his fingers over his moustache, and thinking on Parvati, pulled on the string of his flower-bow with a vow, 'I'll cut the *siddhas* into pieces and burn them with the help of the Mohini Kanya's sidelong glances'. He was confident of his success in wiping out his sworn enemies who had, so far, believed themselves unconquerable.

Just then, moonlight flooded in. Spring was in full swing. The arrival of Mohini Kanya in the assembly of the *siddhas* set in motion a series of most astonishing events. How was it? It was as if Manmath flew wasps among a quiet flock of birds or a deluge of the maiden's beauty submerged the mountains of the fortitude of the *yogis* or ignorance overshadowed wisdom or a cloud of unintelligence covered the rising moon of their intellect or the advent of spring endangered the peaceful lives of the lotuses in bloom or the enchanting appearance of the woman disturbed their quest for enlightenment or a stream of nectar flowing from her lips put out the fire of the yogic practices. The tinkling of her anklets, the melodious voice of crickets, bumble bees and cuckoos and the light of the moon enhancing the beauty of spring induced Ananga to invade a place which he should not. Under those circumstances, the attentiveness of the *siddhas* was broken; their trance dissipated, making way for wakefulness. Their eyes glinted with lust; they felt a strong desire for earthly pleasures.

The Lord was amazed to see the way things were going on there. Holding Parvati in deep embrace, he said delightedly:

Dear me! By what magical powers could you bring Ananga back to life? O Lotus-eyed one! By giving him a new life, you played the role of a creator. Now my anxiety is put to rest. When I was not able to save myself from the hands of Kandarpa, what to speak of the *yogis*!

Mohini Kanya's arrival caused a flutter among the *siddharudras*. Taking a break from meditation, they gazed at her with half-open eyes. Never before had they seen a maiden as beautiful as she was. Scared and delirious, someone resumed his meditation; someone turned to a statue; someone felt as if he was dead; someone was seized with anxiety; someone returned to the state of *samadhi*; someone felt like flying in the sky; someone chanted the name of God; someone got back to the concentration of his mind; someone ran like an *abadhuta*; someone contemplated on heaven; someone was in a hurry; someone was ecstatic; someone meditated in deep devotion; someone was out of sight; someone felt more dead than alive; someone tried to restrain himself; someone felt he and the maiden were alike; someone became passionate; someone clung to his spiritual thoughts, someone identified himself with the woman; someone crossed the boundary of his physical existence; someone thought it was all absurd; someone took it for delusion; someone mistook the rope as a snake; someone considered her the source of energy; someone thought her to be a mirage; someone lost himself in spiritual thoughts; someone labelled it as falsehood; someone elevated his mind to the state of superconsciousness; someone felt the universe in him; someone liberated himself from mundane existence; someone hid his desire for sex like a rabbit; someone thought it was deluge; someone maintained his power of concentration; someone felt one with the woman; someone compared her with an oyster which contained a pearl inside it; someone said it was an illusion created by Indra; someone remarked she had come from the abode of the *gandharvas*; someone said it was the handiwork of Kandarpa, someone said too much attention on her was a waste of time. The *siddharudras*, however, clung to their yogic exercises which they believed would protect them from the three kinds of sufferings.

Among them was a *rudra* named Abhinaba Chaitanya. No sooner did he open his eyes than he fell into Kandarpa's trap. As he fastened his gaze on Mohini Kanya's beautiful face, his mind went blank. His eyelashes fluttered; his heart raced. He was at his wit's end. His body shook and all his wisdom vanished into the thin air. His hair stood on end; he sweated wet. He gasped and a warm blush rose to his cheeks. His eyebrows arched. He was soaking in the warmth of love. His hand-posture changed and his *samadhi yoga* fell apart. Anxiety seized him. His thoughts went wrong. He landed in troubled waters. His hands and feet froze stiff. His senses excited, he was afloat on the waves of lust. Such was his plight.

Mohini Kanya gave a sweet smile, her cheeks going red. She felt that she was going to accomplish her task for which she was born. Parvati's efforts were not in vain. Kamadeva's attempts to lead the *rudras* astray were going to be fruitful. Seeing the signs of victory, he fired flower-arrows at him, which pierced into his eyes. Embarrassed, the *rudra* named Abhinaba Chaitanya was lured into Kandarpa's tricks. Shiva! Shiva! The air in the *sushumna nadi*, instead of flowing upwards, moved downwards. The unfettered elephant fell into the bog of enchantment. Hari! Hari! He broke with the tradition that he was abided by so far. His intellect dissipated, making way for Ananga's temptations. Bewildered, he was unable to tell truth from falsehood. The topmost esoteric point of his mind became defunct. The air stuck to the *nadi* called ida. His quality of unwavering purity was trampled underfoot by the tigress of wild passion. The thunder of lust drilled through the mountain of his forbearance. The maiden's smile, like a *konta*, tore apart the *mahatma*'s spiritual values. The beauty of her eyebrow devoured his peace of mind like a snake eating up the lotus flower. The ecstasy of heavenly joy was replaced by the desire for pleasures of the flesh. The nectar dripping from her lips doused the fire of his spiritual powers. Poor *rudra*! Struck by Kandarpa's five arrows, he was drowned in the sea of sorrow. He had gambled away all his wisdom and fallen prey to Kandarpa's wrath. He had taken leave of his senses by submitting himself to the earthly pleasures. His demure face was speckled with beads of sweat. His lips shook like wisps of hair flopping over the forehead when a mild wind blew. He yawned and tittered. He shook in horror, his eyes set down.

Finding his disciple's reputation in tatters, the Lord told him in a soothing voice:

My son, Abhinaba Chaitanya! You lost your chance of *sidhhi* as your mind is ridden with lustful desires. What to speak of you when that Manmath did not even spare me! Now you will be reborn in a noble-hearted king's house. The earth and the sea will come under your sway. If you take the path of righteousness, you will achieve the attributes of a great *yogi*. You reaped as you had sown. You will have this woman as your wife only when you are born again. Listen! A *yogi*, after his downfall, becomes either a Sambhulinga whom no one worships or a king. Now be prepared to undergo all kinds sufferings. Go and take shelter in the womb of Sashiprava, the chief queen of Ananga Padmakar.

Shell shocked to hear the Lord's words which he knew could not be otherwise, he began to think of birth and death. He considered the earthly life to be nothing but hell. He was reeling from the shock like a banana leaf in wind. His passion for worldly enjoyment disappeared. Realizing the pains of birth, he mused, 'Surely the tigress of ignorance has taken on me'. As he said, he felt like dying. His face fell. His throat became dry and constricted. His courage failed. A great worry was gnawing at his heart. He gave into tears. His voice wavered with emotion.

Broken down with grief, he fell at the feet of the Lord, the Moon-bearer, and, with folded hands, told him benignly:

O Lord! Having served at your lotus-feet for so long, you are sending me to hell for a mistake I committed. O King of the gods! The curse that you pronounced against me cannot be altered by anyone in the three worlds. I told you about the sixteen kinds of sufferings that follow birth. How shall I bear with it? O Lord! You are omnipotent, God of all, all pervading and all-seeing. You manifest in everything, inhabit every soul, the motivator of all actions and the one who can read every mind. Though guilty, I would like to explain in great details the sufferings that lie ahead of the birth process.

O Lord! Mother's womb is where there are heaps of faeces by the river of urine, where the three *nadi*s meet. It has a bladder made of skin and flesh, in which I shall lie, scrunching myself up like a tortoise. What an ordeal I will have to pass! Shiva! The worms will be twisting and turning there, moving on my ears and nostrils while I am entangled by a bunch of *nadi*s. I will bear the pains caused by mother's movement, the growth of bones, the burning of the gastric fire, the harmful effect of rheum, bile and phlegm, the flow of blood, hunger, diseases, deposit of food, the pouring of saliva, the flow of *prana* air and the formation of the seven constituents of the body such as muscles, bones, blood, glands, marrow, skin and semen. I will undergo the three kinds of sufferings of human life. How shall I take in all this? To make matters worse, I will be passing out now and then. O Lord! You push me into a terrible inferno. The more I say about the agony of birth, the more will be left unsaid. Hari! Hari! Once you recollect it, you are done for. The baby comes out of mother's womb through the passage of hell, by the force of wind, on the slippery and stinking path of blood. The baby struggles hard to emerge out of a stream of fluid, overcoming the obstructions caused by bones, the head pushed down by the wind intermittently. It is a crucial situation: On one hand life battling hard to exist and on the other death pulling him hard to finish him off. Buffeted by a strong wind, I would be watching venomous snakes laughing, sticking out their teeth. Collecting myself somehow, and, thinking on God, I would emerge from a narrow, blood-soaken hole like a huge snake coming out of its pit. O God, the Almighty! When I land on the earth, I will let out a cry 'Who am I?' I will drown myself in the ocean of ignorance, gambling away all my virtues. My only concern at that moment would be to know who I am. I would fondly suck a liquid called milk. My body would have been dirty with faeces on it. I would pass through the three conditions of mind: the conscious, dream and the subconscious. O Sadashiva, the Supreme Soul! You will make me suffer all my life, from beginning to end. Hari! Do the gods have hearts made of stone? O Lord! I would spend my childhood in fun and frolic, meaningless activities such as looking after my body, learning irrelevant things from parents and, fearing those who teach me. Next, in adolescence, I would be driven by pride and selfishness which would fill me with grief and remorse. I would experience sorrow, attachment, hunger, thirst, old age and death—the six enemies.

This body will undergo these extreme conditions of life impassively. Impatient and discontented, it will be driven by a strong desire for the pleasures of everyday life. I would suffer from cough and cold. Hope will delude me; the three constituents of material nature such as *Sattva*, *Rajas* and *Tamas* will bind me. I would be subject to the cycle of birth, death and to the bondage of *karma* and its consequences. My life will be mired in ignorance, attachment, wrong-doing, thoughtlessness and illusion. Truth would be a distant dream. Surrounded by the six enemies, I would leave the path of righteousness and consider myself to be only the body. Sans wisdom, peace and love and overtaken by greed and illusion, I would fall prey to Kandarpa and think myself to be everything to me. Dreams, imagination and falsehood would appear to me as the absolute truth. Taking medicine to attenuate my physical sufferings would be regarded by me as a matter of joy. To satiate my thirst I would love taking medicinal drinks and different kinds of food. Does one need food and water when one is neither hungry nor thirsty? When it is too hot in summer we need sandalwood paste to smear our bodies with. In winter, no one asks for sandalwood. To douse the fire of lust caused by Manmath, it requires the company of a woman. A bed is needed for one who feels sleepy. Exposure to fire relieves one of itching. This body is a storehouse of diseases; it needs medicine, drink and proper diet for recovery. It is like mending torn clothes. Birth, old age and death are the stages of life which every human has to pass. Nothing can be achieved without your blessing. As I take body for the soul, I would consider taking medicine to be the most pleasant thing.

O Lord! The woes of youth can't be put in words. A young man is delighted to see the body of a woman which, in fact, is a bag of bones and flesh. He drinks up the saliva drooling from her lips, mistaking it as nectar. He enjoys the beauty of her breasts which are nothing but pouches of skin filled with blood and flesh. He is enchanted by the gestures of her eyes which are no different from water bubbles. Her genitals that he uses during sex are so foul smelling that only worms would love to live there. As a mirage deludes a desert-traveller, these despicable objects, in the name of pleasure, pollute the body and make it suffer. Shiva! Shiva! Had the creator forgotten to cover the body with skin, blood would have been flowing out, insects swarming over it, bones, arteries and marrow exposed. The flesh would shrivel and fats would melt. Crows, jackals, vultures and dogs would be devouring it. Flies would be swarming around it and wild beasts would make a beeline for it. It can't be helped. The body does not stay forever. It is the cause of all miseries. It is an inert object made of flesh and bones. It means nothing; it is the breeding ground of all diseases. It is an easy target of Kandarpa. The nine openings on it exude body wastes. Inside and outside, there is nothing holy about it. It is tied to the three basic components, *sattwa*, *rajas* and *tamas*. I would reap these consequences in my youth.

O Lord! After youth comes old age, when a man's body becomes as twisted as that of a dancer performing on the stage. His hair, darker than the bumble bee, turns as white as Yama's *chamara*. His eyes, looking like blue water-lilies, becomes as ugly as those of a monkey. Overnight, his gold-complexioned body changes into that of a tribal man. His waist, formerly looking like a lion's, becomes as humped as a plough. He will be drooling at the mouth all the time. Some evil power will pounce on his chest. The body turns to a bag of withered bones. The eyes sink into the sockets and the mouth drops. The head shakes like a tree in wind. The navel sinks further into the belly. At every rise, the body gives out a cracking sound and the feet seem too heavy to move. One can hardly laugh without coughing. He is unable to rise from his seat without the support of a stick in his trembling hands. His sensory organs will fail to work and he will be a laughing stock for the youngsters.

O Lord! The craze for pleasure ends in despair. The elements which constitute the body begin to shrivel. Hallucination replaces good sense. The body looks odd and hair falls. There is loss of patience. The head shrinks, goose-bumps appear, pulse quickens, thighs shake, and breathing becomes heavier. Delirious in dreams, the victim lives on liquid diet. His hearing is impaired. Young women make fun of him. His eardrums crack and teeth fall. Having no teeth, he would swallow the best kinds of food after grinding it between the jaw muscles. His mind is polluted, body frail. What an irony! One who used to make gems into a necklace in the darkness of the night is now unable to locate a white bull in broad daylight! He who used to love his wife so intimately for so long, now hates to utter her name, as if it was poison! In spite of having everything—wisdom, generosity, devotion, patience, valour, sense of judgement, good manners, peace, handsomeness, restraint, courage and righteousness, he wasted his youth in pursuit of worldly joy. His childhood was mired in ignorance, youth in lust for women and old age in illness. Like a worm, he becomes the cause of his own death. Life in the womb passed in dirt, midlife in hunger and thirst for lust and last days on bed like a dead body. In such circumstances, how can he win God's favour?

After finishing the story of old age, Abhinaba Chaitanya's thoughts turned to death and the agony associated with it. Suddenly he fell to the ground, unconscious. Regaining senses a while later, he said in a voice laced with grief, 'This sea of life and death is no less than hell. Earthly desires will be of no use to ferry it across. O Lord! I bow at your lotus-feet and wish to speak on the throes of death. Hari! Hari!' His lotus-face, daubed with dust, turned pale and ashen; beads of sweat fell from the sides of his cheeks, a stream of tears splashed down on his chest. He felt himself completely drained out. In desperation, he launched a tirade of abuse at Kamadeva. He felt as if life was ebbing out of him. Lying prostrate before the Lord, his hands folded, he began his say benignly:

O Lord! This body experiences three kinds of sufferings. I could have reached my destination in a few days, but that did not happen. When the time for death nears, one passes out while talking. The eyes look dark and dim and filled with anxiety. Man becomes a victim to restlessness, fear, disease, cough and cold, babbling, misgivings, attachment and weakness. Because of unregulated food habits, fatal diseases arise from his navel. Therefore, the air inside the body becomes still. The disease spreads all over the body, filling it with water. Scared, the fire leaves its place. The air escapes into the *sushumna nadi* to save itself.

The mind, the air and the fire, the threesome, are misdirected into *sushumna* while the components of the body get burnt and the sound of sixteen *damarus* is produced. The pains that the sound of each *damaru* inflicts is severer than the bite of one hundred cobras. The air rushes to the throat causing hicupps that block the passage of the heart. It seems as if someone is hitting the body with a sharp *konta*, obstructing respiration. The elements of the body collapse and the *nadis* enfold the inner content of the head and liquefy it, causing destruction of the elements. It seems like a lion tearing it apart. The area between the throat and the chest is choked with phlegm. As the passage of air is filled with water, the inside air in vain moves upward. Hari! Hari! Seems as if the head will blast. The three humours of the body congest the chest. The huge mass of water drives the air away. The life force, helplessly, rests in the backbone. The *vaidyas* and *yogis* name it as the 'fall in pulse rate'.

When the process of respiration slows down, the body feels a blazing heat. The fire and the air enter *brahmarandhra*, the topmost energy centre located in the crown of the head. They dry up the components of the body. The sound of the *damaru* fades away.

Then, the fire enters the den of illusion. The eyes sink, the passage of the throat narrows down and sweat pours off the throat and forehead. All openings on the body are shut. The water dries up, making way for fire. First, the fire invades the place where the three energy channels or *nadis* meet. Scared, life escapes into Srihattapatana. The fire reaches there, too; then it sneaks into the *sushumna*. At the time *inla* and *pingala nadi*s block their passages. Then, the fire advances to the palate. It is the time when the body loses its external identity and the inner self becomes subject to suffering. The attendants of Yama surround him and torment him, putting a snare around his neck. The flesh-eating demons encircle him. When the fire touches the middle point of the forehead, life prepares to exit the body. All the *chakra*s (energy centres) are set ablaze, along with the mind and the air. The excruciating pain the body feels then is simply unbearable. Thereafter life takes shelter in the lotus with one thousand petals. Still there is no respite for life there as a gust of air pushes the fire on to it. Finding no place to secure itself, life reaches the topmost point of the body, its last resort. Death has no mercy. As the flames rise and touch it, the last chance for life is lost. The being drops, physically and clinically. This is how the journey of life comes to an end. The deeds one accomplishes in the present life determine which womb one is going to take next. The cycle of birth and death continues eternally like the rotation of a wheel.

O Lord! Misled by intellect, attached to *sattva*, *rajas* and *tamas* and lured into Manmath's trick, man would lead hell of a life while passing through the cycle of birth and death. Driven by lust and greed for wealth, he will take the path of wickedness. Polluted within, he will try hard to make his family and relatives happy. He will be mired in ignorance, boastfulness and selfishness. Filled with sorrow and remorse, he will feel himself like an elephant drowned in the deep sea. He will believe illusion as reality, vice as virtue and rot in eternal perdition. Like the boundless sky, he will be upset no end. O Lord! How long shall I have to suffer this way? I have served you all my life, Don't I deserve salvation? Won't it be an act of injustice on your part to deprive me of it?

Abhinaba Chaitanya took a pause. His hands folded, he looked at the graceful face of the Lord and said his prayers in fifty alphabets, each prayer beginning with one alphabet:

'Shivaya namah! Shiva! Shiva! Shiva!'

You are adorned with flowers such as *kunda* and water-lilies; the complexion of your body is as white as camphor and throat shaped like a conch. A garland of red water-lilies around your neck, you have a skull in your hand, snakes around your arms and a deer skin wrapped around your waist. Your eyes are like blazing inferno. Earrings of most poisonous snakes on your ears and all over your hands, you are the founder of dance form. The soles of your feet are as soft as buds. Your abode is the Kailas. You are the destroyer of Kamadeva. O Supreme Soul! You smear the Mountain's daughter's breasts with *kumkum*. Karttikeya, Brahma and Kamala's consort worship at your feet. Decked in crown, earrings and serpents and carrying a *damaru* in your hand, you are the glory of the kshatriya clan. Calm in heart, you have mastered the art of awakening *kundalini*. You have matted hair and eyes as divine as lotus. Your abode is located in the golden mountain. You have no inclinations to have earthly pleasures. Your complexion is as white as the Milky Sea. You carry an unwieldy trident, as hard as the shell of a tortoise. You are merciful to the young women who pray to you with great respect. You are as terrible as Yama. Kamala's consort serves you; both of you are parts of the same soul.

O Lord! You wear the moon as your crown. You are armed with *khatvanga* and axe. You travel across the sky unhindered. You have no clothes on you; you are friend to the Garuda rider. You have drooping eyes. Your consort carries a cutlass in her hand. Glory to you, O Lord, the ruler of heaven! Your appearance is like that of the sky. You carry Ganga on your head. Half of your body is that of Girija. You are the protector of cattle. Always in a yogic posture, you are surrounded by your followers. You are father to Ganapati, God of knowledge. Your throat is blue because of the effect of poison. Your eyes illumine when you chant Gayatri. You ride a bull; you pat it on its cheeks. You are the Lord of cattle. You are the Lord of Ganga's life. You have a graceful gait. You are an epitome of virtues. You look terrible when you pull on the *pinaka* bow. You reside in the five-petalled lotus called *sahasrara*. You are truth incarnate. Calm and composed, you have tamed your senses. Your lotus-feet is worshipped by all. The beloved of the daughter of the mountain, you look as radiant as the blue water-lily. You are a friend of the Lord of Nilachala. Lakshmi's consort worships you. Your body has a golden complexion. You represent the highest state of intellect. You are most considerate. You have a tranquil heart and a steady mind. Worshipped by the Wheel-bearer and loved by the moon-faced Goddess, you burnt Kamadeva into ashes. Your eyebrows look like a bow. You are head over heels in love with Parvati. You are the Lord of the fourteen worlds whom sixty-four *yoginis* pray. As a *chakravaka*'s eyes are fixed on the moon, your eyes are locked on the moon-like face of Chandika. Your complexion is like those of Ananta cobra and the moon. You have wrapped the world in the shadows of illusion.

Glory to the Lord of the universe, who protects humans from the agony of rebirth. Your matted hair looks like the waves of the Yamuna, Yama's sister. You are Uma's consort; you liberate human mind from worldly bondages. You preserve the creation; you destroy it. You are the cause of deluge. You look as radiant as fire. You are the Lord of Beasts, the protector of the earth that extends up to the sky. Loved by the consort of the daughter of the sea, you dispel ignorance. A great *yogi* yourself, Ganga flows from your head in three streams. Worshipped by all, you protect the humans from hell. Your face looks like the moon; a chant of your name washes away all sins. Nanda's son admires you. Decked in snakes, you are the mightiest of all. You protect the righteous. O Parvati's consort! You don't stick to one place. You contain the whole creation and all the gods in you. O Propounder of *yoga!*

Glory to the Lord who carries *damaru* in his hand. The creator of the egg-shaped fourteen worlds, you dwell in the topmost esoteric point of the body. Lord of the universe, you are attended by the *yogis*. You are the destroyer of the demons. O Five-headed Lord! You carry Ganga on your head. You are formless, protector of the virtuous. You endow your devotees with divine powers. You are the ruler of forty-nine crores of islands on the earth. You are the rider of Suravi's son. You burnt Kamadeva with the fire from your third eye. You killed Andhaka. You give no consideration to caste. You devour the forty-nine winds. You overpowered Ananga. The liberator of souls, you are the Lord of the three worlds. You remove all kinds of suffering. O Trident-bearer! Basuki cobra rolls around your head, which is fifty crore times bigger than the earth, You outlive time. You are omnipotent. Half of your body belongs to Parvati. You are the creator of *sattva, rajas* and *tamas*. O Moon-bearer! You are the creator of all. Your body is as soft as lotus. You are in deep love with Mountain's daughter. You are always lost in meditation. You contain the land, water, fire and wind in you. You are adept in all tantrika practices. You possess eight supreme divine powers.

Glory to you, O Lord, You punish the wrong-doers. With angry eyes and surrounded by the messengers of death, you look as deadly as the forest-fire. A great *yogi*, you preside over the ten directions. You are the slayer of Daksha and the demons. You are worshipped by Devaki's son. To see you is to achieve salvation. You are the redeemer of all sins and destroyer of Daksha's *yajna*. You are the mightiest of all. You killed the demons who considered themselves to be invincible. Your eyes are like the sun and the moon. You redeem the sins of your devotees. Dear to Damodara's heart, you are cruel to the evil-minded. You look as radiant as twelve suns. O Merciful God! You bless your devotees with boons. You destroy your foes effortlessly. Half of your face is shared by Parvati. You wiped out the clan of demons. You are like the daylight in the dense darkness. You are the remover of poverty and squalor. Ever merciful, you ward off the power of evil.

O Lord! You are lost in meditation ever. You are the cause of meditation. You are preoccupied with it. Propounder of *yoga*, you are *yoga* itself. You hold it as a treasure. You are meditative in body and mind. *Yogi* of *yogi*s, you are the root of the ways of *yoga*. You are the preserver of the earth; you look after it with love and care. Your body represents the earth. Like a bumble bee you suck honey from the lips of Mountain's daughter. You pervade the whole earth. Extremely patient in nature, you smear your body with ash that makes it look smoky. A comet to your foes, you are the benefactor of the earth. You are of white complexion; you ride a white bull; you carry the white-looking Ganga on your head and stay in a snowy mountain. You are the symbol of consciousness and dispeller of ignorance. You carry the crescent moon on your forehead. You are the incarnation of *dharma* who does not discriminate between good and evil.

O Lord! Your eyes look like the new cloud, except the third one which is too mysterious to comprehend. You are the Lord of kings, *naga*s, Ganga, Nandas, *rakshasa*s, wealth, beasts and Nilachala. You are the purifier of the energy channels. O Creator of nine kinds of worlds! You are the mightiest. You outlive the deluge. You are omnipotent, the holiest and greatest of all the gods. You are always in a state of ecstasy. You are the liberator of mankind, the Supreme Self on whom Vishnu meditates. You manifest yourself in the three worlds. The slayer of Kamadeva, you dwell in the five constituents of creation. You are *Brahman*. To you the remote and the proximate are alike. You pervade the nether world and heaven. O Parvati's consort! You are the symbol of peace and light. You took the poison emerging from the churning of the sea. You are the spirit and the nature, both. At the same time, you are none of these. You are not bound to the senses. You put on a garland of lotuses and are adorned with snakes. Brown-eyed, you make friends with Pandu's sons. You are Paramahamsa. You sit on the lotus of fifty petals while in meditation. Your throat is shaped like the Panchajanya conch. You are worshipped by the wise.

O Lord! Snakes are your earrings, sacred thread, wrist belt and arm bands. They create a hissing noise all the time. Lord of sages, you fulfil their heart's desire. You are Vivasvata, the Lord of those who are in pursuit of enlightenment. You are the cause of creation. O the mightiest! You inhabit the Vivasvata constellation. You are *Brahman*, as invisible as Vivasvata. Bards sing your glory; the gods bow to you. You are respected by the great sage Vasistha. Garlands around your neck, you are not led by senses. Your eyes look like forest fire; you destroy the most deadly weapons. The mighty ones bow to you. You are the Lord of celestial women. O the slayer of Vasudeva's enemies! You are as swift as a storm. O the Bull-rider! You are the destroyer of worldly desires called *maya*. You are the Lord of the gods and *gana*s. You are a friend to Varuna. You don't differentiate between the young and the old. Buddha, the son of the earth, Brihaspati, Indra, Vivasvata and all the grahas worship at your feet.

O Lord! You reside in the mountain with the Mountain's daughter. You are all-pervading. You dispel illusion and ignorance. Bhargava, the sage, worships you. Your head is adorned with Ganga. As a bumble bee loves flowers, you love the lotus-face of Bhagavati. Your eyes glint like the sun. You are surrounded by supernatural beings. O Bhadresvar, Bhavani's consort! O Bhairava! You have no mortal feelings. Your body is adorned with snakes. You are the cause of the creation as well as its destroyer. You remove the sorrows of the earth. Fortunate are those who serve you. You never discriminate between fortune and misfortune. You judge people on the basis of their *karma*. You represent the five primordial elements of creation. Protector of the universe, you are dispassionate and detached from worldly affairs. You smear your body with holy ash. The earth is like a girdle around your waist. Krishna serves at your feet.

O Lord! You are Madhava, the creator and the destroyer of illusion. You are sinless to whom the sages pray steadfastly. You carry Ganga on your head. You are adorned with a garland of *malati* flowers. O Mahesvar! Vishnu worships at your feet. You kiss the nectar-filled lips of the slayer of Mahisasura. You are beyond human comprehension. Clad in tiger skin, you look as terrible as Bhairava, You travel across the Western Ghat mountains. A foe to Kamadeva, you are the greatest mind of all times and the mightiest of all. Benevolent and blissful, you have a garland of skulls around your neck. You are the *mantra*, the conqueror of death. You are the liberator of all souls, whom Vishnu worships. You are static and self-born. A great *yogi*, you are the Lord of the sages. You are the creator of the world which is as delusive as a mirage. You perform the most terrifying dance form, *tandava*. You are the swan of Manasarovara. You have followers at your service. Your body is as radiant as the fire on the Meru and the Mandara mountains.

O Lord of the universe! You are the life-giver, a *yogi* in *samadhi* posture, like the moon of wisdom that makes the lilies of the minds of the *yogi*s bloom. You are averse to rituals. You are invoked in *yajna*s and, also the destroyer of it. You remove the suffering associated with birth process. You are the well-wisher of the world and redeemer of the fear of Yama's snare. You are Yogesvar, the propounder of *yoga* whom sage Yajnavalkya meditates on.

Glory to you, O Lord whom Ramachandra adores. You reside in a beautiful cave. Your eyes look like lotus flowers. O Mahesvari's consort! You bear the moon on your head. Your body is as white as the moon. O slayer of Kamadeva! Your three eyes symbolize night, day and evening. You look like a red lotus. You are King of kings. You love and, at the same time, hate sensual pleasures. O slayer of Rati's consort! Vishnu, lying on the ocean bows down to you. You contain all *rasa*s. You are fond of flowers. Each of your hair-root contains a universe. You are formless. Your body is as radiant as one thousand suns. You are more handsome than Kamadeva. Rukmini's consort prays to you.

O Lord Haladhara! You have no feeling for shame. To you, gain or loss has no meaning. You place the moon on your forehead. The mountain is your abode. You are the Lord of fourteen worlds. You are an epitome of virtues, not attached to *maya*. Your hair-roots contain the water of the first deluge. Sage Lomasha worships at your feet.

O Lord! Your lips are as red as *badhuli* flowers. You inhabit the *brahmarandhra*, the highest point after the six *chakras*. The crescent moon is your crown. You have instilled in man the feelings rising from the sensory organs such as mouth, hand, feet and bones. Your belly is the sea, arms thunder, thighs and feet the earth, face the *Brahman*, eyes Vaivasvata, words Sarasvati and body the universe. You are the redeemer of sorrow whom the three Vedas admire and Brahma meditates on.

Glory to Chandrasekhara, Sarangadhara! You are the source of peace. You look like the Autumn moon. You sit on a seat made of deer skin. You are the consort of Parvati, the doe-eyed one. You have on you auspicious signs such as conch and lotus. You are dear to the Wheel-bearer's heart.

Glory to Shiva Shambhu who leads the life of a *yogi*, with the moon on his forehead. You represent consciousness and purity of heart and mind. Your hair is adorned with snakes, so also your waist. O Shankar Shiva, Shakambari's consort! Sri pays her respect to you. Your hands, feet, throat and voice have a divine touch. O Sripati, the source of energy! You reside in the mountain peak. Your glory cannot be put in words. You are worshipped by Sri Ramachandra. Your earrings hang over your cheeks. You are non-partisan in your judgement. You sing Samaveda all the time. You are attended by female ghosts. You are as illusive as a rabbit's genitals. Shukra bows to you. You have command over lustful desires. You are the deluge, all-pervading.

O Lord, the creator of Satya Yuga! You perform six rituals as enjoined by the Vedas. You are mentioned in six *shastras*. You dwell in the six-petalled lotus. You are served by sixty-seven crore of *apsara*. You have sixteen divine attributes. Well-versed in hundreds of *shastras*, you know how to operate the six *chakras*. You are father to the six-headed Karttikeya. You are the source of six *rasas*. You are well-versed in the six branches of the Vedas. You are invoked with six rituals.

O Lord, the Motivator of all actions, who bears all auspicious signs! You have renounced everything. You are the symbol of spiritual joy and the one who fills all with happiness. You have no form. You are Truth incarnate. You exist for all eternity. Lord of the illusive world, you are detached from *maya*. You are the Lord of the three worlds, you inhabit all souls. You are worshipped by Sarasvati and all supernatural beings. You outlive time and appear in many forms. Radiant-looking, you possess one thousand hands, one thousand feet, bellies, waists, thighs, ears and noses. You exist for one thousand *kalpas* and dwell in the lotus with one thousand petals. You are as respectable as Salagram. You pervade the water, sky and fire. You are Ganga's consort whom you carry on your head. You are the redeemer of the sorrows of the world. Nothing hides from your view. You are served by celestial nymphs. You are the Lord of the seven rivers and seven universe. You destroy the seven elements of human body. You are worshipped by seven sages and the sun who travels in a chariot to which seven horses are yoked. You carry on your head a snake with seven hoods. You are benevolent to the seven worlds. You are alone and, at the same time, you keep a large company. You dwell in seven mountains spanning over the seven worlds. You are Parvati's consort. You are *Brahman*, the purifier of *nadis* and *chakras*. You are worshipped by Sage Shuka.

Glory to Shiva Shambhu! Haladhara! You are fierceful, the Lord of celestial nymphs who dwells in the Himalayas. Consort of Mountain's daughter, you have a complexion as white as snow. You are ever joyful, adorned with necklace and bracelets. You are benevolent. You don't discriminate between good and evil. You inhabit the lotus-heart of Hari. Your eyes are as radiant as fire, body like fire, soul like fire. You stay in fire, you are all in flames. You devour fire. You are Lord of fire-worship, the supreme soul. Clad in deer skin, you are kind to the doe-eyed women. You are the lotus among a flock of swans. You are the propounder of *hatha-yoga*. You have a complexion like a diamond. You are the one who is invoked in the performance of horse-sacrifices. A garland of skulls around your neck, you are calm and composed. O Lord of the Himalayas! You give no consideration to loss and gain. You always keep chanting Hari's name. Both of your hands are of equal length like those of the elephant. Clad in elephant skin, you are the one whom the sun respects.

O Lord! You don't discriminate between the transient and the permanent. You are the Lord of the *ganas*. You are the sea of compassion, all-forgiving and all-pervading. A great kshatriya as you are, you are the cause of the creation of the three worlds. You are neither hungry nor thirsty. You travel across the Milky Sea. You are not interested in pleasures transitory. Redeemer of all sins, you are represented by the idols of eight Lokanathas. O Lord Shiva! Pardon me.

O Lord! You have no beginning. You are invisible and inscrutable are your ways. O the Supreme Soul! You are immortal. Your glory is beyond human comprehension. O Soul of souls! You are adorned with Ananta cobra. You are the Lord of the eight clans of *nagas*. Half of your body belongs to Parvati. You are self-born. You are redeemer of all fears and you bestow eight kinds of divine wealth on man. Slayer of Ananga, you are inexhaustible, sinless and remover of all sins. O Ambika's consort! O lotus-eyed Lord! All the gods worship you. Sage Astavakra meditates on you. You put on a garland of skulls. The horizon is where you live.

O Lord! You are a wonder. You can spread yourself up to Brahma's abode. You contain the whole universe. Lord of land and sea, you sit on a red lotus. You have no beginning nor middle nor end. You are the redeemer of the three kinds of sufferings caused by the world, by the gods and by self. You outlive the deluge. O life-giver! Your body is as vast as the sky. You exist for all eternity. You are Universal Soul, always ecstatic, whom Indra's consort honours. Puranas sing the glorious history of your life. You have the power to confer the position of Indra on whomever you choose. You are the propounder of the ways of *yoga*. You are benevolent. O God of gods!

Glory to Uma's consort, whose love for her is immense. You represent 'Ukara'. You remove all obstacles that arise during a *yogi*'s meditation. You are adorned with a spectacular garland. You are an epitome of virtues and the greatest benefactor. You don't have clothes on you. Redeemer of sufferings, you reside in Udayagiri. You look like the rising sun. You are free from the agony of birth and death. The snakes roll all over your body. You live in the north.

O Lord! The sages worship at your feet. You have no form. *Rigveda* sings your glory. You are immutable. You are always engrossed in yogic practices. You are well-versed in *tantra*. You are Vishvesvar, Bhubanesvar and Rupeswar. You are fond of visiting Ekamra Vihara often as a resort. You are the eleven Rudras taken together. Decked in Shesanaga, you are one and many. You are the giver of the divine powers. You are worshipped by the Lord of Airavata and Goddess Lakshmi. You are the creator of the world of illusions.

O Lord! The four Vedas are on the tip of your tongue. Ananta Deva is on your lips. You are all-pervading. You bear the moon which is the source of all medicine on your forehead. You are the symbol of all cures. You are the cause of illness and its attenuation.

Om is the symbol of *Brahman*. You are *Om*. *Om* means the soul as the self. The sound it produces rises from the fourth of the six *chakras* in the body.

Glory to you, O Lord, the Preserver and the Destroyer. You are omnipotent, formless and incomprehensible. O Lord of all divine powers! You are Achyuta and Ananta. Half of your body is shared by Ambika.

CHAPTER 2

Sashiprava Conceives and the Arrival of the Abadhuta

Having finished his prayers in fifty alphabets, the *rudra*, Abhinaba Chaitanya, lay prostrate before the Lord. Impressed by his disciple's extent of wisdom expressed in humble words, Sadananda, the Merciful, said in a voice bathed in nectar:

My son, Abhinaba Chaitanya! Why do you fret so much? Can misfortune befall someone as learned as you are? Nevertheless how can one get away with doing something wrong? Birth and death are indispensable for every living being and you are no exception. Your *karma*, prompted by your earthly desires, ended up in wrong-doing. Consequent upon the sin you committed, you are liable to suffer the agony of birth and death. This is how you will have to pay for your sin, which the Vedas call *prarabdha*. Now you will be born again and lead your life as luxuriously as Lord Indra does. In the long run you will receive God's blessings. To the north of the western seashore, at the foot of the Himalayas, there is a city called Basudha Mandala. It is in Kanchanakara kingdom on a mountain peak, next to Dadhimanthara city, by the River Amrita Tarangini. This city is immune to sorrow, poverty, old age and untimely death. The king of the city is Ananga Padmakara who has a minister named Bibeka Ratnakar. The king's chief queen, Sashiprava is virtuous and as beautiful as the Mahendra mountainous range. She is past her youth, and, being issueless, has been praying to me since long to have a son. A descendant of a respectable clan, the king is as just and honest as he is righteous. There has been no untoward incident nor injustice nor calamity in his land. Indra used to rain in his kindom generously. Like King Yudhishthira of olden times or like Kubera, Vishrava's son, he is resourceful in all respects. In spite of having everything, he is unhappy as he has no issue. To restore the peace of mind, he has been performing many religious rites as enjoined by the shastras. What are they? They are observance of daylong silence, *chandrayana*, exposure to heat and cold and living on fruits and roots. He used to invoke Manmath for help very often. He is in full control of his senses. His wife has been with him always, participating in all activities. At the end of each Karttika and Magha he would meditate standing on one foot, his hands upraised. He propitiated the five kinds of fire called Panchagni and he used to live on grass juice and *bel* leaves only. Indifferent to heat and cold, he would hold holy grass and water in his hand day and night. He pleased the gods and ancestors with offerings and fed one crore brahmins after washing their feet.

He engaged himself in eight parts of *yoga* including *samadhi* and performed religious activities such as pilgrimage, planting trees, digging ponds building shelter-houses, mutts, *mandapa*s, gardens, sinking wells, building temples entertaining guests with great hospitality, performing *yajna*s, arranging annual swearing ceremony and providing food and water for his subjects. Wishing for a son, he made charitable offerings to the poor and needy. What were those offerings? Those were land, water, food, clothes, ornaments, houses, elephants, trees made of gold, *purusa*, *yamaghanta*, Hemagiri *mandala*, Amruta Bipula Tira, potful of sesame seeds, gold, curd, conches, cows made of gold, one thousand young women decked in jewellery, beds, mats, land such as *kshetra*, *pura*, *sasana*, *nagara*, *patana*, hills, rivers, forests, potful of ghee, trees made of gold, gems, *salagram*, secret gift, milchy cows, deer skin and herds of animals. In addition, he paid some money to them. He had been performing a *yajna*, wishing for a son, which would end that night. In fact, his wishes were fulfilled on the day he first chanted my name, but I had to keep him waiting as I did not find the right man to become his son. As his son, you will rule the earth. The king is worthy of becoming your father. He is known for his forbearance and righteousness. He is well-mannered, omniscient, noble, brave, kind, peace-loving, generous and benevolent. He is a Vaishnava and of good conduct and character. He is well-versed in the Vedas, pure in heart and mind, conscientious, wise, just and a great kshatriya. He is steadfastly loyal to me. His fame is spread across the length and the breadth of the earth. I told you all about the king. Abhinaba Chaitanya! Now get going. Don't delay even for a moment. Shelter in queen Sashiprava's womb. Bear with the sufferings for quite some time.

The Lord commanded Mohini Kanya to go and become King's Dharmadhvaja's daughter.

Carrying out the Lord's command, Abhinaba Chaitanya bowed to Goddess Parvati and sat in lotus posture. Of the sixty-four types of *yoga*, he chose the one called Taraka Dhatu *yoga*. He united the *nadi*s such as *inla*, *pingala*, *sushumna*, *alambusa*, *kaukshani*, *gandhari*, *hastijihva* and *sankhini* with many other *nadi*s such as *naga*, *kurma*, *krukalaka*, *debadatta*, *dhananjaya*, *apana*, *vyana*, *samana* and *udana*. He, then, directed the energy called *kundalini* to the lotus at his heart, in the shape of Om. He filled it with *prana* air, which rose like the flame of a lamp from the *trikonagni mandala*. That flame touched the *kundalini*. Just then, as a potter's wheel produces pots out of a lump of earth, the energy began to revolve around the navel. Passing many energy centres (*chakra*s) it touched the most sensitive part of a female body. It was like adding fire to a pot of ghee to melt it. The circulation of the energy with the help of the inhaled air created a body out of a lump of sperm called *dhatu*, with hands, legs, nose, etcetera. This process is called Taraka Dhatu *yoga* in which a life is created with all physical features, like the air containing all kinds of smells.

This way that live sperm entered Queen Sashiprava's womb and got trapped in it, like *kamahansi* held captive by Manmath. At the time the queen was asleep in the arms of the king on her gem-studded bed. Suddenly she got up frightfully. Shocked, the king traced his fingers over her body to comfort her. He asked her in a soothing voice, 'O moon-faced one! What makes you so scared?' The queen explained, 'I dreamt that I was neatly dressed and my hair braided. The three humours of my body such as rheum, bile and phlegm were in order. My mind was calm. Do I have anything to worry when you are there with me?' The king consoled her, 'O dear! The night is about to end. We will talk more on it, O doe-eyed one, in the morning.' The king and queen, after having a wash, took their seats. They spent the rest of the night talking on Krishna's life.

Soon it became light. The eastern sky glimmered with vibrant colours. The gem-necklace became as cold as fog. The light of the lamps dimmed. Darkness hid in holes. 'Awake!' The hen called out her daughter. The betel inside the mouth tasted bitter. The breasts of young women lost their warmth. The stars in the sky disappeared. The *chakravaka* smiled. The *yogi*s took to meditation. After breathing exercises, the *yogi*s, who used to take food only at the sunrise, went out for collecting alms in the city. The *sannyasi*s took to *pranayama*. The bumble bees left sucking honey from the water-lilies and set out for lotus forests. Seeing the bees covered with the pollen grains of the water-lilies, the lotuses swung in the morning wind, blushing. It seemed as if they were unwilling to entertain the bees. The owls retired to dark places. The air was filled with the sound of conch. Lustful women freed themselves from their husbands' grip. Thieves felt unhappy. The men who guarded the city at night retired to bed. The moon faded into insignificance. The cocks crowed. The cowherds left for the meadows to graze their cattle. Children went to *chatasali*s to learn. The women who had been to their paramours returned home. Rati's face looked as cheerful as that of a woman after having sex in tiger pose. The supernatural beings disappeared into the dark. The summits of the mountains were clearly visible as light fell on them. The gods took their positions in the Meru Mountain. The lotuses of the *apsaras*' breasts looked as if daubed with musk. Feeling shy to look at their chests, the *gandharva*s washed them with the water of the Mandakini. The boatmen left for their boats. Those interested in physical exercises left for the *akhada*. The women, whose husbands were away from homes, kept count of the days of their return.

As it became light, the queen left her bed. After bath, she offered water to the Sun-god. Then, accompanied by the king, she reached the place where the *pundit*s had assembled. Standing aside, she started narrating her dream to them. How many kinds of *pundit*s were they? They were of sixteen kinds. Some were old by body, some in knowledge, some in age, some in their ability to influence, some in manners, some in devotion, some in learning, some in contentment, some in patience, some in *siddhi*, some in humility, some in renouncement, some in principles, some in benevolence, some in truthfulness and some in the sense of judgement. They were self-controlled, detached from worldly affairs, men of words, self-sufficient, averse to sensual pleasures, steadfast in devotion, righteous, Vasudeva's devotees, respected in their area, engaged in pursuit of knowledge, well-versed in *shastra*s, always joyful, worshippers of Shiva and Vishnu, Paramahamsas, austere and soft-speaking. Again, how did they look like? Perfect in shape and size and sagacious, they were clad in yellow clothes, with three lines of ash on their foreheads which symbolized the destruction of *sattva*, *rajas* and *tamas* by the fire of their wisdom. How beautiful the grass-rings on their fingers looked! Did it help them control their earthly desires? What for they adorned themselves with nine strands of sacred thread? Did it stand for the nine kinds of *bhakti*? Did the beads in their crystal rosaries remind them of the illusive world of birth and death? Or they counted the beads considering that in spite of leading an austere life, they were subject to rebirth? To redeem their past sins, they had garlands of *rudraksha*, *tulsi* and coral around their necks. How lovely the garlands looked! Did that represent their learning and *tantrika* practices? All of them knew how to control their senses. They had no greed for food. They were friendly and pure in heart and mind. They were truthful, soft-speaking, patient, kind and well-versed in *shastras*. They used to settle disputes as instructed by the *shastras*. To them the chief queen called Sashiprava, whose face was like the autumn moon, eyes like blue water-lilies, gait like that of an elephant, breasts full, waist thin, complexion fair, looks enchanting, nature virtuous, hips protruding, glances charming so as to attract the gods, lips smiling, body smeared with fragrant cosmetic, voice like cuckoo's and walk like that of a swan narrated what she had seen in her dream, from her chamber that looked as dazzling as the sun made of nine gems.

O *pundits*! I bow to you. Please listen to what I saw in my dream carefully. At the crack of dawn when I was enjoying a nice sleep and in a relaxed mood I had a dream. I was neatly dressed and had my hair done. I had no problem with my bodily humours. My mind was calm and undisturbed. At that time a strange thing happened; a radiant-looking figure entered my womb. How was he? He looked as white as crystal, like Lord Shiva. His eyes were like red water-lilies, his eyebrows as arched as a swarm of bees or the waves of the Kalandi, face like the full moon and earrings like Jupiter and Venus. His flowing matted hair was hanging over his chest. He was looking as radiant as the jewel on the hood of a great snake. His body was smeared with ash, looking like the sun or the moon emerging from behind a plume of smoke. He had a tiger skin around his waist. He had shoulders like those of a lion, long hands, large eyes and ears and a solemn look. His lotus-eyes were full of ecstasy. As the *mahatma* entered my womb, I felt a twist of alarm inside me.

At this, her voice skidded to a halt, as if a string of Manmath's harp got snapped, bringing an abrupt end to the music. The *pundits* drank in the nectar dripping from her moon-like face with rapt attention. Consulting the *shastras* dealing with dreams, the learned *pundits* said to the king:

Your Majesty! Fortune has smiled on you. The virtues of your past life would never go unrequited. You planted a tree of *dharma* on the soil of your noble actions. Its roots lie in the devotion to Vishnu, its top in loyalty to Rudra, the trunk in the purification of the soul, branches in an equalitarian mindset, buds in the externalization of conscience, leaves in *yajna* and other religious rites, bark in benevolence, juice in compassion, aerial roots in doing good, hollow in an ideal family life and flowers in dedication to Vasudeva. Now it's time the tree of *dharma* bore fruits. A great Shaivite *yogi* has taken shelter in the queen's womb. He has to experience all the pains related to the process of birth. He has come in response to your prayer to Lord Shiva. As he failed in his duty, Lord Shiva has sent this *yogi* here on punishment. Astrologically the dream has nothing inauspicious about it. The queen is fortunate enough to bear this child. It will wash away all her sins. O king! Your son is a great soul who excels in everything. He will be as handsome as Kamadeva. He will rule over the land and the sea. He is the incarnation of *dharma*. You will be proud of having him as your son.

Glad to hear it, the king offered them many gifts for their services and washed their feet in respect before they left for their respective places.

Once they left, the king mused, 'May their words come true!' To ward off evil spirits he gave away a lot of donations. As days wore on, many changes appeared in the queen's body and expression. Her face looked like a lotus collected long ago. Her body had an unhealthy pallor. Her chest shrank and belly swelled. Her nipples looked darker like lotuses surrounded by bumble bees. Her eyes, as beautiful as blue water-lilies, now looked dim and sticky. The bangles on her hands loosened. Her waist-belt became too short to tuck the garland of flowers into it. Her lips lost their lustre, as if *badhuli* flowers were rotting in ash. She felt sick. It pained her as she walked. She liked to have cold food only. Her navel like the stalk of a wood apple fruit now bulged out.

That divine sperm formed its base in the womb and got stuck there. It was like a lotus seed germinating inside a beautiful pond. Without being harmed by the gastric fire, the foetus lay on a net-like bed inside a bag of skin, supported by the cord supplying food to it. With Vasudeva enshrined in his heart, thinking on the Ultimate Reality, keeping his concentration intact and realizing the ways of *Brahman*, he wished to have a human body. He lived on the air flowing through his anus which was called *apana*, while his mind was entirely focussed on God. Unable to bear with the pain which was inevitable, the queen broke down with grief. The fear of the unknown seized her. Her complexion looked whitish. She had a headache very often. Her hair-roots swelled. She lost interest in food. It was too painful for her to walk. She suffered from constant vomiting. Her breathing became heavier. Clothes fell off her body. She wished for more rest and no work. Her belly itched. She lay on the bed, her face up. Her body looked like a crushed betel leaf. Her voice, as sweet as that of a cuckoo, turned hoarse.

Finding the queen in such a woeful state, the king was extremely worried. After purifying himself, he sat on a crystal *mandapa* and performed a *puja* meant for wish-fulfilment. How was it? To begin with he created in his mind a clear sky beneath the seven worlds and filled it with the light of crores of suns to purify it. Then, he imagined water above it, considering it to be flowing from Vasudeva's sweat in form of nectar. With that water he began the worship. That sea of sweat contained the whole universe. He imagined a lotus growing from Vasudeva's navel. He, then, purified the universe with the nectar flowing from it. In this universe called Padmabhaba he placed an imaginary tortoise and meditated on it, taking it for God Almighty. What was the tortoise like? Its back was as hard as thunder, eyes like the rising sun, tongue like the lightning, nails like the half-moon and belly as dark blue as the cloud. Sitting in lotus pose, he worshipped it. Its breath contained all the seven worlds. Next he imagined eight elephants. What did they look like? One was like the Himalayas, another like the Kanchan mountain, the third like a roaring fire, the fourth like a massive crystal, the fifth like the evening cloud, the sixth as if made of gem, the seventh of the complexion of smoke and the last one like the Meru Mountain. They had four tusks each.

Thus he imagined eight elephants, and concentrating his mind on them, he worshipped them with incense, lamps and food with recitation of *mantras*. Decked in finery, the elephants were holding a frog with their tusks. What was the frog like? It was immortal. Its body was as rough as a blue stone; it had the mark of sacred thread on it that shone like a rainbow, its eyes were as radiant as planet Mars. He had created such a frog out of imagination and worshipped it ritualistically. The same way he imagined a lotus flower on its head, the stem of which measured sixty thousand hands. That was a full blown flower, ever bright. It was made of gold, the wind wafted away its fragrance across quite a distance. It had one hundred petals; it was called the lotus of the nether world. On it, Lord Ananta was seated. The king began meditating on Ananta cobra, who looked like molten gold. It had coiled up around the lotus and was in deep meditation. Its eyes were as radiant as the sun. It had one hundred hoods, the gems on them shone extremely bright. Decked in blue clothes, it had adorned the golden lotus. The king, then thought on Basuki. Reciting *mantras* from Purusasukta, he sprinkled some water from Ganga and performed the *puja* for wish-fulfilment. Of the one hundred hoods the serpent had, the middle one was the largest. The crown it wore shone like the sun, atop it was a piece of gem in which the earth reflected like a sesame seed. The king worshipped the earth for its purification, offering incense, lamp and food. He then, imagined Lord Ganesha to be on its right, his *gurus* on its left, Lord Krishna above it and worshipped them all. He also worshipped Kala Bhairava, Yama, Indra, Maruta and Kubera, placing them on his four sides. He purified all parts of his body as enjoined by *yoga*. First he purified his body from feet to the thigh regarding that part as the earth, from the thigh to the anus as water, from anus to the navel as fire, from the navel to the heart as wind, from the heart to the throat as the sky and from the throat to the head as *Brahman*. Returning to the lotus, he finished praying to Sri Ganesha and Goddess Hakini. Then, turning his face to the west, he bowed to Lord Shiva, reading out Rudra *mantra*. Next he prayed to Narayan placing him in the *svadhisthana chakra*, the lotus in his heart. Then, he worshipped Sarasvati imagining her to be seated on the sixteen-petalled lotus. He also worshipped the sun and the moon and the Goddess of sleep. As he invoked Lord Shiva seated on the one thousand-petalled lotus in the *prana chakra*, he heard a voice calling out to him, 'O king! The day an *abadhuta* comes to your place and meets the queen you will be relieved of all your worry. He will bring comfort to your son in the womb, who is none but myself.' Hearing the voice, the king ended his *samadhi* and returned home. Since then, he kept waiting for the *abadhuta* to arrive.

There came a day when the *abadhuta* reached the king's palace. What did he look like? He was dark brown in complexion, his matted hair was of golden colour. His eyes were round and brown in colour. He was fat and tall. He had a loin-cloth around his waist and his eyes were wide open. He was heavily drunk. As a practitioner of Kulisha *yoga*, he had achieved excellence in *pranayama* and the control of *inla* and *pingala nadi*s. To him, the seven vital constituents of the body did not matter at all. He had command over many yogic practices. He knew how to activate *kundalini*. He went without food and sleep. He had attained *siddhi*. His body smeared with ash, he looked quite impressive. He had conquered the fear of death.

The *abadhuta* considered the seven seas to be just a pollen grain, the forty-nine airs a single breath, the earth an atom and the sky a snake. He had taken it for granted that the whole world was in his control. He had been counting the gods among insects.

He thought that Brahma, Vishnu and Mahesvar were passing miserable lives. His hair was ruffled, body daubed with ash, inside clean and shining. He had a stick in his hand, a piece of loin-cloth around his waist and a dead snake as his sacred thread. Living on some sacred roots, he had hung the rim of a broken earthen pot from his neck. He was carrying a potful of rice on his head. He was walking unsteadily; it seemed as if he was in a state of insanity. He would condemn the most delicious food offered to him and would pick the left over food from the ground and eat it. Once he sat in meditation, he would continue it for twelve years. Lest he might be accused of vanity, he pretended to be a devotee of *Brahman.* He was extremely self-centred, which showed his ungodly approach to *yoga.*

Led by his senses, the *abadhuta* entered the city, walking like a lion. He had not yet enjoyed the real spiritual joy as he was still clinging to the desires of earthly pleasures. Therefore, he was still subject to the cycle of happiness and sorrow. Though he spent his time in meditation and prayers, going without food and sleep, he was returning to the world of senses very often. He lived secretly in a cave in a hill. He envied any good advice. He pretended to be fearless, but he was afraid of achieving anything bigger. Scared of the wind on the way, he used to cover himself with a cloth mattress and did not speak to anyone for fear of diminishing his spiritual power. He was proficient in *tantrika* practices, but was deprived of spiritual joy as he had no faith in Vishnu.

As he reached the Lion-Gates, the king caught sight of him from the platform he was sitting on. Seeing the king, the *abadhuta* grinned at him, considering him an animal. Reminded of the voice he had heard during the *puja*, the king bowed to him in respect. The *abadhuta* teased him, 'Have you taken leave of your senses, O king? why do you bow to someone who is much younger than you are?' The king replied, 'I hold you as my God. God inhabits every soul. Lord Shiva dwells in the cremation ground. He blesses his devotees when pleased. You are my God.

It is but for the virtues of my past life that I could see you!' At this, the *abadhuta* asked, 'Tell me, what you are worried about'. The king replied, 'O Lord! My chief queen is carrying; she is unable to bear the pains she is having'. 'Let me see the queen', he suggested. The king led him along the way to the inner palace where the queen used to stay.

The king offered him a golden bed, studded with gems to sit on. How was the bed? It shone as bright as the sun. Its legs glittered like the moonbeam. Clusters of pearls were hanging from it which looked like the stars. It was a lovely bed covered with a sheet as white as foam. It was strewn with the petals of chrysanthemum flowers and sprinkled with camphor dust. As the *abadhuta* took his seat, the king had his body smeared with *aguru* and sandalwood paste and offered him many gifts. He adorned him with expensive necklaces and fanned him to relieve him of the pains he had taken to come there. He served him with milk, rice and coconut juice. Pleased with the king's hospitality, the *abadhuta* sat there hand in hand with the king. Another bed was laid for the queen to sit on.

Looking as depressed as Goddess Earth when oppressed by the wicked, the queen, accompanied by the king, entered there with slow steps with her maids. Hiding her body in a green saree, she came, all the while thinking on Narayan. How did she look like? She looked like the full moon peeping through the evening clouds. Such was Sashiprava whose gait was like that of a swan. As she took her seat, the *abadhuta* remarked, 'Hey, you are carrying a great *yogi* inside you. He must be either a *siddha yogi* or a *yogi* fallen out of God's favour. Now we will know the truth.' Saying so, he sat in lotus pose, and, concentrating his mind on the lotus of his heart, he adopted the yogic method to enter another body. He recited some *mantra*s and reduced his body to a molecule, which contained all the features of human body such as the five vital airs and ten sensory organs. Then, he emerged out of his nose, intending to enter through the left nostril of the queen. He said to himself, 'Let me enter her womb and locate which *mahatma* is there inside'.

With this in mind, he came out, leaving his body behind on the bed in a state of *samadhi.* As he tried to enter through the queen's left nostril, he backed out like the bees flying away from the light of the lamp realizing that it was not a flower, but fire. He bowed to the queen and mused, 'How is her body so hot!' To facilitate his entry, he blew some *apana* air into her right ear in an invisible way. The *apana* air, as cold as the moon, brought down her body temperature instantly. Soon she fell asleep on her bed. By that time she was seven months pregnant already. The Yogesvar inside the womb sensed some change happening and became alert. He was all ears for any sound coming from outside. He awakened his consciousness and revived his past memory. Just then the *abadhuta*, staying at the queen's earlobe, called out 'O *mahatma!*' three times. The *rudra* inside the womb thought: I hear a human voice. Who is it? Not Vishnu because he would display his *maya* only after I am born. Is it Shankar calling out to me to awake? Let me talk with the caller. Again he thought: the voice I hear is imperceptible to human senses. It appears to be a talk between some creatures and ants. If that is so, I must have heard other voices too.

With this in mind, the *yogi* made a sound. What was the sound like? It was like the soft melody of a flute or the feeble sound of a young cricket or the sweet sound of a female parrot. Thus the *yogi* spoke from the womb, 'Hey, who is it addressing me as *mahatma*? It is stupid of him to do so. Do the *mahatma*s rot in hell as I do? You may say the soul and the body are two separate things. It matters little to me. I am just a living being. Had I been a *mahatma*, would I have said these words? Should a *mahatma* experience birth, death, fear, illusion, sleep, sorrow, attachment, fever and ignorance? How can I be a *mahatma*? I am not so. I am a fallen being. Have mercy on me.' This he said in a quiet voice.

His words surprised the *abadhuta.* He wondered, 'How fortunate I am! Today I shall extol the virtues of learning many things from him. I have never heard such things before.' He, then told the yogi, 'My son! Are you a *sidhha yogi* or Lord Shiva himself? Listen to my words as sacred as nectar. My son! I have been an *abadhuta* all my life. Today I will fill your mind with delight. Don't make your mother suffer any longer because of the excessive heat your body emits. Be cool. Whatever boon you wish for, preserve it in your memory carefully. How could such a wise man as you are fail to attain *siddhi*? You are scared of taking a human form. You are seized with anxiety when you hear my words. In which form are you now? How do you feel? Tell me all this. I will ordain you as my disciple soon after you are born'. The *yogi* thought: A human being can never be God. This must be a man of little learning. He seems to have attained *siddhi* through *tantrika* practices. He is boasting of his achievement. He is egoistic in nature. Let me ask him about his thoughts and intentions. Let me discover what lies in his mind. I must find out whether it is his compassion or *maya.*

Wrapped in such thoughts, Abhinaba Chaitanya, the *rudra*, asked him, 'O Man! Where are you speaking from? What do you see around you? What are you thinking about? Answer to my queries.' The *abadhuta* replied, '*Mahatma!* I am on the earth which appears to me as an object. It is wrapped in illusion which manifests in everything. There is nothing greater than it.' Hearing this, the *rudra* asked, 'What kind of object is the earth? How does it look?' The *abadhuta* replied, 'It is made of solid and hard substances. It's a huge land mass, the whole of which one cannot see. It is situated down below.' The *rudra* interrupted, 'What do you mean down below?'

The *abadhuta* said, 'How can you understand unless you know what is above? Well! You need not worry about it now. Just know that the direction in which the *prana* air flows in the *sankhini nadi* is called above. It is from there that your voice comes. The direction in which the *apana* air flows is called the middle. The earth exists there. It is surrounded by the sea which is vast and deep, filled with foam and froth, where the waves rise and fall. It is of blue complexion. Up above there is an object called the sun. The stars shine like the jewels that are found in elephants. On the earth time is determined by night, day, month and season. The wind blows over it. There are many creatures living on it having one, two, four and eight feet. There are millipedes, men, demons, *gandharvas* and *kinnars* in it, too. One of the seasons is meant for rain. Another strange thing is that during the rains the lightning flashes from nowhere and the rumbling of thunder is heard. Sometimes there is hailstorm too. The sky is another strange thing; it appears in many colours such as white, yellow, green, red and brown. Living beings like us inhabit the earth. Sometimes we are awake, sometimes in a state of dream, in which the being in us sees many strange things. There is also a state of unconsciousness in which we are oblivious of what is going on around us. This is how the body works.'

'What is the body?' The *yogi* asked.

The *abadhuta* explained, 'It's quite mysterious. The body is a solid mass composed of twenty-four elements. There are nine openings on it. Above them, there is a hard object called head which has a tuft of hair on it. There are two big openings down it that look like water bubbles. We see with it; it is called the eye. On its two sides, there are two holes known as ears. We hear with it. When they are blocked we don't hear anything, but only a whizzing sound. Between them there is a structure looking like a bird's beak; we call it nose. It has two nostrils which are the passage for the flow of air. When it stops taking air, we die.'

'How does a man die?' asked the *yogi*.

To which the *abadhuta* said in answer, 'All attempts to save life fall through. The body begins to decompose. It disappears into the earth I was talking about. There will be no trace of it any longer. *Shastras* are of the opinion that the deeds of a man's past life determine which womb he will take next.'

'What is *shastra*?' the *yogi* asked.

'That which tells wise words,' said the *abadhuta*. 'We listen to it with our ears and recount it in our hearts. Below the nose, there is a big opening called mouth; we speak with it. That one is the biggest door on the body. It is surprising that it has hair around it, like the fence around a disused well. Inside it, there is a semicircular trap-like structure made of bones which we call teeth. There is a tongue inside it which acts like a monkey and looks like a snake. It is always greedy for delicious food. It gives out a bad smell if not washed by water regularly. Down it, there is a narrow passage called throat. Down below are our hands and feet which are comparatively thicker than other parts. This is all about the parts of the body. To feed the five constituents of the body the mouth fills itself with food and sends it to the energy centre at the navel through the throat. Air pressure plays a vital role in pushing the food down. The gastric fire called *jatharagni* burns near the navel invisibly. Usually water douses fire, but this fire burns brighter when it comes in contact with water. It cooks the intake of food. The residue excretes through the opening meant for faeces and urine. This is how the body functions. Driven by the desires of senses, man experiences joy and sorrow in his life.'

Hearing this, the *yogi* said, 'You are mistaken. That the world is full of illusion is nothing but one's ignorance. Only *Brahman* pervades the whole earth. Things seem otherwise to you because of your ignorance. Everything that you said is inside every soul. It appears different when seen from outside. These misgivings misguide your senses. It is only your imagination that arises from your dreams. Your viewpoint is absolutely wrong. Ignorance interprets illusion as reality.'

Those words took the *abadhuta* by surprise. He became more conscious of the soul than the intellect. His pride vanished.

Dumbstruck, he told the *yogi*, 'Tell me all that you see there. Do you see day and night? Can you know when your mother is awake or dreaming or sleeping?' The *yogi* replied, 'For some days I saw nothing and knew nothing. I had no idea about the world or about myself. I had no knowledge of who I was or what I was to become. In the beginning I used to hear a sound like that of a bumble bee when it enters a hole in the wood. Gradually it developed into many kinds of sounds. I had no control over it. I can't say how the creator, the cause of *maya*, did it. Remembering how I lost my former life, I had been able to come so far. When wind in my mother's belly blew in gusts I knew she was dreaming. When her *nadi*s vibrated, I knew she was talking. It pained me when she changed her sides. I could not bear with the pain when the womb was too hot or too cold. Sometimes more air flowed into my ears and nose. Sometimes the darkness changed into light which you may call day. The memory of my past life filled me with sorrow. When my head was downcast, I knew my mother was walking. Sometimes my head used to move eastward or southward; it did not stay steady at one place. Then, something uncommon happened, a surge of happiness having no reason. It gave rise to the reasoning faculty and self-consciousness and I felt a sense of loss.'

After a pause the *yogi* continued, 'In this world, dream is mistaken as *siddhi*. Once born, man clings to illusion in form of the nature around him. It scares me. The world presents only a reflection of itself like a mountain in the mirror or a banyan tree in its seeds. One considers the reasoning faculty to be pure and absolute. That is how Vishnu displays his *maya*. It is like the waves mistaken as sea. *Maya* is the product of the reasoning faculty which subjects human life to the cycle of birth and death. O *mahatma!* What should I do to free myself from ignorance and keep my memory intact after I am born. Tell me if you know.' The *abadhuta* advised him, 'My son! *kundalini*, the coiled up energy centre at the navel, represents wakefulness which comes from consciousness. Ignorance rules supreme if *kundalini* is in a dormant condition. Once it is awake, air will begin to flow in the seventy-two thousand *nadi*s. If one is a bit careful one will never be a victim of ignorance.' Hearing this, the *yogi* said, 'Well! Let's see what you said is right or wrong. I also think that ignorance is a form of *maya*. *Maya* is the creator and the destroyer of the world. Time and nature gather strength from God. They serve as God's maidservants. By meditating on God one can awake *kundalini* and stay away from ignorance. Darkness does not exist when the sun is there. The *shastra*s say the same thing.' The *abadhuta* was amazed. He said to himself, 'I don't believe a child in the womb saying all this! Is he a *dikpala* or some God who has descended on the earth to establish the law of *dharma*?'

Deciding to gather some confidential information from him, the *abadhuta* said to him, 'O the person in the womb! I felt no joy in attachment. Manu says that the only way to attain salvation is to take the path of righteousness. It is selfishness on two counts. One: the pains one has to take to adopt *dharma*. Two: the sorrow of imagining the existence of the other world which is the best place to live in. The Samkhya says the soul is free and independent; it has nothing to do with senses. The wish for heaven brings grief and despair. One cannot obey the dictates of senses for long. According to Patanjali there is nothing called reasoning or knowledge which we call consciousness; it is only *maya*. If it be true, there will be no difference between man and animal. It is neither good nor of any use. Mimamsa says in God's opinion *karma* brings sorrow and suffering to man, even God is no exception. Look at Lord Shiva. He travels on a bull with a *damaru* in hand. He dwells in a cave in the Kailas. He has no lust nor anger. He bestows men with all worldly happiness. He has a family with wife and children. He suffers during the deluge, though he is always in a state of *samadhi*. This is nothing but sorrow. Of what use is all this? In the opinion of Vaishesika the world is a house of animals; God is not there. Where, then, is the room for happiness? According to Kaumari Vishnu is the universe. The nether world is his feet, the seas his belly, the sky his body, the seven worlds up above his crown, the sun his eyes, the hollow in the nether world his nose, the forty-nine winds his breath, *dharma* his ears, Yama his tongue, Sarasvati his words, Brahma and Indra his arms, Lord Shiva his mind and Mahamaya his motivator. Accepting him as God Almighty, we will meditate on him. This is the idea behind the creation of man, but what is the outcome? The Pashupatas are of the opinion that the world is a combination of Shiva and Shakti. The moon is Shakti and the sun is Shiva, the soul Shakti and God Shiva, the earth Shakti and the Meru Shiva, the ocean Shakti and sea-fire Shiva, the air Shakti and the mind Shiva and the mind Shakti and consciousness Shiva. With this in mind, you may go on working till you die, but you will gain nothing. *Nyayashastra* says only God is there, nothing else. If it is true, there will be no cause for sorrow. How does it matter if God only exists or if man clings to human passions. According to the science of logic the universal soul, like the sky, pervades the whole creation. Should one, therefore, meditate on the sky and pray to be part of it? It makes no sense at all. According to Buddhism nothing can be done without body and that body is where all passions are stored. If so, what is the use of body, then? It indicates that both the body and the soul are meaningless. On one hand the soul does not exist, on the other the self causes painful consequence. The anahata theory explains that soul is the truth. It gives rise to knowledge. What pleasure is there in gathering knowledge about the things around you if you are to die in the long run? According to *tantra* purification of the body can be done through Yoga. It can create miracles such as flying like a bird in the sky, which has nothing to do with religion. What success is there in flying like a bird in the sky? Doesn't a vulture do it? This is a false interpretation of God. The popular belief is that the *prana* air and the reasoning faculty are interconnected. Therefore, one needs to continue with the *prana* air, failing which death will overtake life. Those who are past youth mistake the individual soul as *Brahman*. They make the stupid argument that the soul in man is of no use if it cannot differentiate between dream and reality. The soul, like a lamp burning, exists in the middle of the body. What sense does it make for a man to focus his attention on it all his life? The followers of the Shakta cult say that whatever remains after forgetting everything is the soul. According to the Upanishad the only thing that exists in the world is consciousness, which is the reflection of the soul. But, has it got anything to do to make one happy? The Vedantic view is that the knowledge of *Brahman* means everything—joy, piety, fearlessness and the quality of unwavering purity. It keeps one's mind in an ecstatic state of complete bliss and love. It does not happen in a state of dream. It's like making a herd of asses move round a central post to which they are tied. All grope in the darkness having no idea of reality. According to Chintamani whatever one meditates for, one achieves it. Well! No one is greater than Brahma. So meditate on Brahma and become a Brahma yourself. But, what is the use of having four heads? Riding a swan, one will have to remain busy creating one thing after another. One day one will pass away, suffering from pneumonia. Does it make any sense? The practitioners of these theories will have to die at last before knowing the real meaning of *dharma*. Driven by their ego, the sages formulated their own views and put it on record. After a pause the *abadhuta* implored, 'My son! Tell me where to find God in his real form. You are my guru. Have mercy on me.'

It seemed the *yogi*'s words had a terrible impact on the *abadhuta*, to the extent that he realized his own mistakes. He thought his earlier attempts to know the truth were futile. Driven by a demonic desire to drink in the nectar of spiritual joy, he had vainly followed various paths he had cited. Hearing his words, the *yogi* thought: At last the light has dawned on him. Deprived of divine grace he had been thoroughly disappointed. He said to the *abadhuta*, 'O *mahatma!* The views you quoted here seem one and the same to me. The learned ones know it. Each of these contains the essence of wisdom. As you had not realized the truth, you tried them, one after another. True knowledge comes to those who are as hardworking as an ant, who meditate on Vasudeva and renounce the desire for earthly pleasures. You are devoid of self-realization as your mind is not pure and still under the control of *sattva*, *rajas* and *tamas*. Listen to me. The happiness of Indra, Chandra, Surya, Rudra, Brahma, Vishnu, emperors, Daksha, *gandharvas* and ten *dikpalas* taken together cannot be equal to that of the realization of the Supreme Being.

Listen to how great the Supreme Being is. Because of our illusive mind we see a distorted picture of the universe. He is omniscient, omnipresent and omnipotent. He pervades the entire universe. What you consider many is, in fact, an atom to him. He is absolute and incomprehensible. Do you understand? Will plants grow if seeds are sown on a stone? That can happen when we sow seeds on a tilled land. You are just an anvil. How can you understand it? The steps that lead to self-realization cannot be put in words? It can only happen if the disciple develops an interest in unfolding the mystery. Words fail to describe the one who is beyond the comprehension of the mind and the intellect.'

Hearing this, the *abadhuta* said, 'I have been a *yogi* for seven thousand years. You are a foetus. I ordain you as my *guru* and worship at your lotus-feet. Be kind to me. Tell me how to know the Ultimate Reality.' To this the child in the womb replied, 'A *guru* cannot impart all the knowledge to his disciple at one go, likewise it is not possible to revive your conscience at one stroke. As a king conquers kingdoms one by one, not all at a time, you have to train yourself through many stages. Now on you take the path of righteousness without expecting anything in return. Meditate on Vasudeva with steadfast devotion. In time Rajas and Tamas will disappear. Only sattva will remain with you. With purity of mind, you will have to cultivate the qualities that are considered virtuous. What are they? They are giving up ego and violence and adopting peacefulness in your conduct. Pay respect to your guru and purify your heart. Keep your mind calm. Have patience. Control your senses. Always remember the agonies of birth, death, old age and diseases. Take refuge at God's feet. Detach yourself from everything. Concentrate on your soul. Live a secluded life. Treat everyone equally. Be truthful. Do as I say. Cultivate a sense of devotion in you. Don't make friends with anyone. Don't be in love with anything. If you follow my advice, you will develop a spirit of renouncement in you. This sense of detachment is called conscience. You will never be fascinated with the things around you. This world is an illusion. By applying your conscience you will be able to distinguish between the transitory and the everlasting. In this phase you will argue with yourself. About what? You will debate on whether sickness, enjoyment, wealth, body and impediments are true. If not, then what is the truth? Conscience never lies. It knows all material things are as repelling as hell. Once you know it, you will renounce everything.

There are four kinds of asceticism: *shruti*, *kamala*, *raga* and *praudha*. Among these *praudha* is the best. A *praudha* ascetic is the one who rejects the world-from grass to *Brahman*-like one vomits out the undigested food. He leaves his house and spends his life in a hermitage in meditation and prayers. The spiritual practice is of four kinds: *shanta*, *danta*, *uparati* and *titiksha*. No desire for material things and clinging to what is just and true is known as *shanta*. Total renouncement of earthly desires externally and internally is called *danta*. Detaching oneself from worldly affairs, yet feeling happy and contented is called *uparati*. Indifference to joy and sorrow, fear and safety, profit and loss, good and bad, vice and virtue, success and failure, cold and hot, praise and blame and victory and defeat is known as *titiksha*. One who masters these four deserves to be the right claimant of self-realization. Serving religious gurus and listening to scriptures will wash away all your evil thoughts. You will feel completely detached from the world of senses. This feeling cannot be put in words. In this condition, the more you see others, the more you forget yourself. This indifference to your body is called reverse thinking. God manifests in all living beings. The *atman* considers the world nothing more than an object. The body is not the soul; you have not yet realised this. You consider your wife, sons and relatives your own. Once you know the truth, your reverse thinking will be there no more. Thereafter, be cautious about what you hear and what you think. Listen to the *shastras* attentively. It is like hearing the *guru's* words. When you are convinced that all are one and the same, you complete the first leg of your spiritual quest. In the next phase you will be inclined to ask yourself: Who am I? Am I the world or the sky or the senses or the life or the intellect or consciousness or the three qualities of nature or water or fire? It is the third phase when you go for yogic exercises. Constant practice of *yoga* is called daily meditation. The fourth phase is known as Bijayini. What is it? In this phase there is no desire for anything. That you say you are not happy is because you are still a victim of desires. The foundation of ignorance is as strong as the Meru Mountain. It has taken the whole world in its grip. Unless and until you experience peace, you won't enjoy eternal happiness. This phase leads to all other phases like all things emerging from the Milky Sea. All your desires and ignorance get dissolved in the soul. The fifth phase is when you are in the state of *samadhi* in which the meditator and the object of meditation are united. *Maya* comes in many forms to cast its spell on you. It uses all its might against the *yogi* in form of fear, attachment and unconsciousness. The mind rotates like a whirlpool. It makes the *yogi*'s devotion to Vasudeva sterile and trap him in eighteen kinds of illusions, called Vishnu's *maya*. What are they? They are awakening, dream and unconsciousness. Besides, there are other divine illusions that overpower the *yogi*. They are Mohini *maya*, Madhumati *maya*,

Bisayavarnini *maya*, Sabdamayi *maya*, Sarasvati *maya*, Debayoni *maya*, Animadi Ascharya *maya*, Jalandhari *maya*, Laukika *maya*, Kamayi *maya*, Siddhamayi *maya*, Kallolini *maya*, Rudrashankar *maya*, Parvati *maya* and Sarvamanohari *maya*. This way the eighteen kinds of *maya* surround him. *Ascharya samadhi* is like a dream when the mind is free from all earthly desires. When one is in a state of divine bliss with his senses dissolved within, like a lamp that has been put out, the concentration of the mind rests on *trikuta*, an imaginary point inside the forehead, located between the two eyebrows. There, time, the destroyer, leads the mind to a state of unconsciousness. Once these *maya*s are conquered, the *yogi* takes the path of lifelessness when the mind becomes dead. It is then that the divine *maya*s appear. The sages, the gods and the *siddha yogi*s know it. They are seduced by many such forms of *maya*. Even Brahma and Shiva could not protect themselves from it. You may say when they failed, what about me? Jagannath is the creator of Maya. Without his blessing no one can accomplish the task successfully. He fulfils the wishes of his devotees. He is all in all in the matter.'

Hearing this, the *abadhuta* said, 'O *mahatma!* Tell me the role played by the different forms of *maya* in a *yogi*'s life.' The child in the womb interrupted, 'I can't talk any longer. It's bed time for me now. Let me answer to your query in short. To gratify your request and for the benefit of others I am telling it. It will help you assuage your grief. Some *maya* may ascend you on the throne of Indra and make you Brahma. Some will provide you with the company of thousands of women. Some will make you travel in the sky. Some will offer you divine chariots to move about in the sky and enjoy a life like that of Indra. Some will enable you to talk to the gods. Some will let you know the news of the land one thousand *yojana*s away. How much shall I say about the delusions they display? Even it is beyond the God's comprehension. Those whom God blesses can understand it. After the different kinds of *maya* are neutralized, comes the sixth phase in which the *yogi* is brought to the state of deep unconsciousness, which is *turiya.* A lot of voices arise from within. When, gradually, the voices melt down, a flame appears as bright as the light of crores of the sun, the moon and the stars taken together. As the flame disappears, a clear sky appears in its place. Within that sky there is another sky called chid, which is very compact. This comes as the seventh phase, when the real happiness is felt, making the *yogi* realize the *guru*'s words. This state is called *nirvana.* There is unlimited joy, nothing but joy. It has no end, like the waters of the sea. It is that joy which Brahma and the other gods pine for and which is still beyond their reach. If you abide by the rules, you will attain salvation which means Vishnu's blessing. *Yajnas*, *puja*, charity and pilgrimages are meant for it only. The Vedas sing its glory. The gods crave for it. Once you take refuge at Vishnu's feet, the deluge of crores of universe seem to you as extremely insignificant. To you time becomes meaningless. Words fail to describe Vishnu's glory. Do as I say and meditate on Vishnu.'

Feeling relieved, the *abadhuta* lay at the feet of the child in the womb, whom he accepted as his *guru.* Then, he sought his permission to take leave of him. He assured the *yogi*, 'I vow to do as you say'. The *yogi* said, 'I will take my birth in a short time. I will be in meditation and observe silence. My mother will feel comfortable from today. Now let me have some sleep. We will see each other in the Kalinjan Mountain.'

Returning to his former self, the *abadhuta* looked at the king. At the time the king, dumbstruck, thought: How strange! He was in *samadhi* so long. How come his body like that of a dead man, keeps shining! The *abadhuta* stepped down from the bed. He held the king's hand and whispered in his ears, 'From today your queen will be relieved of all pains. She will be blessed with a brilliant son.' He paid respect to the king, considering him his *guru*'s father. He was exceedingly happy to have extolled the virtues of hearing the child's words, as sacred as nectar. He took his leave and left for the forest. Thereafter the queen awoke, feeling happy and relaxed. Her face lit up; it seemed as if the moon was released from Rahu's grip. Seeing her sorrows gone, the king was quite relieved. Filled with joy, he gave away charitable offerings to his subjects to ward off the evil spirits.

CHAPTER 3

The Birth of Rudra Sudhanidhi

Days wore on. It was the third day of the bright fortnight of Vaishakha when Queen Sashiprava gave birth to a baby. It was Cancer *lagna*; Jupiter was in the house of Moon in central position; Mars was in the seventh house; Mercury and Venus held auspicious positions while Saturn and Sun were highly placed. The planetary alignment was quite propitious. The horoscope of the baby showed the signs of a bright future such as acquiring wealth, power and fame.

On such a day the baby was born. He was fully conscious when he left his mother's womb and landed on the earth, as he was remembering Vasudeva all the time. When the fateful moment arrived *apana* air flowed downwards, the *nadi*s turned to the left, the seven vital components of the body were activated and the abdomen lowered down. Seeing this, he concentrated his mind on *brahmarandhra*, the highest energy centre at the crown of the head and meditated on Vishnu. Saying 'O Lord Vishvanath, the Moon-bearer! I bow at your lotus-feet,' he emerged out of the hellish womb and fell on the earth. For the purification of his soul he performed *pranayama*. Thinking on Vishnu, he imagined the seven worlds to be on fire. He created twelve imaginary suns and burnt the forests, mountains, rivers, seas, creepers and houses. Thus he destroyed the whole universe by fire. He, then, imagined sixteen moons rising. He created imaginary rain clouds and caused heavy rain that submerged the fourteen worlds with water, foam and froth. He meditated on water for a moment which he imagined to be ages. Then, he created sea-fire and turned himself to fire. Next, he meditated on the wind which filled the bodies of all living beings. Turning himself to wind, he destroyed the wind by wind. He created a clear sky and felt himself as the sky itself. He waited for a moment which seemed to him as ages. He thought the sky to be Ananta whom some people called *Brahman*, others the Almighty. Then, he created the Nature of which *sattva*, *rajas* and *tamas* were known to be three chief qualities. With *sattva*, he formed a sky in his mind. From the sky the wind was born; from the wind came fire that caused the birth of water and from water the earth was created. He created a new universe, and, invoking Vishnu, he redeemed all his sins. Thus he purified himself and the earth.

As narrated in the Puranas, there was a Yogini of Mahesvari's clan whose name was Sutaka Harini. She used to visit the earth off and on to take the lives of those who were newly born. That's why Goddess Sasthi used to guard the babies day and night. In spite of it, Sutaka Harini succeeded in her mission when she found a chance. Therefore, no one in the world should claim a child to be his own. Out of fun, she used to look for babies all the time. Attracted by the sight of the newborn, she rushed to him riding a golden post, as the dark cloud was attracted by the lovely moon. She stole the lives of the elderly people in the palace and tied those lives to the end of her saree in a knot. Then, she prepared herself to take the baby away. How did she look?

Pitch black in complexion, she had big and brown eyes rotating like a wheel; her tongue was like the lightning; teeth like the crescent moon; large eyebrows and breasts were hanging over her knees. She was dressed in black and had her bun decorated with *landabaguli* flowers that looked like a flock of storks. Her waist was like a *mridanga*, lips as black as *jamun* berries, eyebrow like a black snake, eyes sunk deep in sockets, hair on her body like molten gold and belly shrunk to her back. Her voice was like the sound of a broken bugle. In such a form she arrived to take the baby's life. When she bent over him, it seemed as if God of Death had come to pull away a dead body with his snare.

Seeing her, the baby thought: who is this witch? I have seen many *yogini*s attending Parvati in the Kailas, but none of them is like this one. She is bent on capturing me. With this in mind, he invoked Parvati and sat in a yogic posture called *meru-mudra* that made his body firmly glued to the ground. As she caught him and tried to lift him, the baby did not budge an inch. She tried again and again, letting out a loud roar that made her face, eyes, ears and nose bleed. When all her attempts to carry him away fell through, she decided to kill him.

Sensing what was going on in her mind, the baby burst into laughter. Hearing his sweet voice, Sutaka Harini was taken by surprise. Dumbstruck, she stared at him. An unknown fear seized her. With a deep sigh, she said to herself, 'Least afraid of the gods, men, *gandharva*s, *yaksha*s and *kinnara*s, I accomplish my task at my will. I have never seen a baby, just after his birth, laughing like this! Didn't God tell me earlier that I can't harm Vasudeva's devotees? I think he must be a Vaishnava. Otherwise how did I fail to raise him when mountains used to rock at my cry? Let me engage him in conversation and enquire about him.' But before she could have a start, the baby said, 'It is Ketu *maya*. I don't see anything wrong with you. Why are you so enthusiastic about taking this wretched body of mine? Driven by your vile nature, you have stooped so low! How can you be so inhuman? Looking like a witch, you have filled your life with sorrows and sufferings, but pretending to be a merry soul. You do things that are abominable. Why are you in a tearing hurry? You try to lure the queens into your tricks. Your ignorance propels you to resort to violence. What pleasure do you derive out of it? You don't know what would be best for you to do. You regard the living beings as of no value. No other person is as distressful as you are. How can you have the real joy? Like the beauty of a *malati* flower in the forest, your youth is simply wasted. You will make your life better if you go to the Kailas and serve Parvati there. Because of your cruel nature, people call you Hidimba, the demoness. I take pity on you. Now it's time you gave up your wicked nature.'

Sutaka Harini said, 'My son! I feel fortunate to hear your words. Today is the luckiest day for me. You changed my mind. You must be an incarnation of God. Why don't you laugh once more? Why don't you show your face, as beautiful as the moon, to me? Why don't you dispel the darkness of ignorance from my mind? Why don't you give me some advice to comfort my soul? Why don't you unfetter me from the shackles of mundane life? Don't I consider everyone as lowly as grass? Why don't you rain the nectar of your advice from your lotus-face down on me? Why don't you part the curtain over my eyes that had blinded me? Why don't you accept me as one of your disciples? Why don't you liberate my soul? Why don't you teach me *pranayama?* Why don't you be my *guru?* Greed for wealth is a form of illusion. Let me conquer my senses. Let me be free from the sorrows that spring from water, fire and bodily humours and make myself happy. How I wished I had a peaceful and prosperous life!'

Convinced that Sutaka Harini's aspiration for spiritual knowledge was genuine, the child-*yogi* took pity on her. With a smile on his lips, he said, 'Oh! What makes you so wise?' She replied, I used to listen to the religious discourses among the sages and the gods. I wished to have the spiritual joy which the gods including Indra and Brahma crave for. But I didn't find a *guru* to guide me. Please have mercy on me. Save me from the mire of ignorance.' At this, the baby told her, 'That depends on your *karma.* As a man, faint with hunger, does not eat food with both of his hands, your prayer would not be heard so quickly. Now on you look after me as my nurse. Wait for my advice until I grow up. Keep chanting Vasudeva's name. That is the mother of all spiritual knowledge. All knowledge comes from it as everything emerges from the Milky Sea.' Saying so, he fell silent.

Right at that moment she shed off her terrible form and changed herself into a beautiful woman. Her hair brown, undone and ruffled now looked as black as the waves of the Kalandi. Her body of dark complexion changed into a fair one, smooth and polished, like the middle petals of *champaka* and *ketaki*. Her ugly face looked like the autumn moon. Her look became enchanting; her eyebrows like black snakes looked so beautiful as to put Kandarpa's bow to shame. Her nose looked like a sesame flower; her crooked eyes became as beautiful as blue water-lilies; her teeth like the crescent moon earlier, now looked like *kunda* buds and her lightning like tongue looked like petals of water-lily. What to speak of her ears? With earrings on them, they assumed a lovely look. Her voice which was as harsh as that of a broken bugle sounded as sweet as that of a male cuckoo in spring. The *landabaguli* flowers she had decorated her bun with was now replaced by scented flowers. Her breasts hanging over her knees now looked like the protuberances on both sides of a young elephant's brows. Her legs like those of a stork appeared as inverted banana trees. Her gait looked like that of a swan. She changed her black clothes into white.

In such an appearance, Sutaka Harini served the newly-born as a nurse. She untied the knot of her saree and released the lives of those she had stolen. Getting back their lives, the elderly people awoke and found the queen had given birth to a baby. A loud cheer went up among them, which was as deafening as the sound of the sea. They had the baby bathed with the water collected from many holy places. The king gave away land, money and cows among his subjects.

All were pleased to see Sutaka Harini looking after the child. They said, 'Sasthi Devi has arrived to look after the king's son'. The baby was regarded as the full moon shining over the Milky Sea of the king's clan. Queen Sashiprava's heart bloomed with joy like a water-lily. The clouds of sorrow that had overshadowed the king's mind had by now, disappeared. His son was the apple of his eye. The event had silenced his enemies both outside and inside the court. The step mothers were exceedingly happy to see the child. The king's mind, like a ship, was afloat on the ocean of joy as his worries had come to an end. It was like a poor man coming across a lot of wealth or a blind man getting back his eyesight or a lustful man acquiring the knowledge of hypnotism for everlasting youth or a lame man being able to walk or a man wishing for the redemption of his soul achieving his goal.

Lost in joy, the king rewarded the storekeepers, performed *yajna*s and commanded that the subjects be allowed to do whatever they liked. They were given a free run even to rob the stores and markets. As the news was announced all over the kingdom, the traders were excited. All the greedy and evil-minded people such as Huria, Taria, Thenta, Ganthia, Thieves, Juara, Pokhad, Porthia, Liha, Lulumpa, Chatua, Ghatua, Lekhua, Lenka, Lambahata, Natua, Margala, Balia, Hatua, Batua, Thatua, Kathua, Mathia, Sathi Daudia, Regada, Dhandua, Bola, Pela, Pahantia, Dhenka, Matua, Badua, Khechada, Puruna, Madua, Jhamalia, Tahimela, Takeria, Randua, Hugulia, Hathiora, Melia, Mandobasa, Bibhasolia, Phasiora, Phatia, Bandhra, Kharadanga, Kharadia, Khanjeria, Bharia Dhada, Dharida, Dhaba, Tuthua, Utautha, Begadia, Muhapoda, Dhuda, Dhulidhumpa, Dhoura, Pakhia, Pakhalakhia, Bheta, Pelapelipasha, Agatabola, Gilua, Dahana, Damarakoa, Dangara, Roga, Rogakuha, Barnahina, Takarakhia, Chhaila, Chhanchunia, Dahana, Golia, Nasikabihina, Pempala, Kaunria, Chharia, Thonthada, Pindabasa, Taka and Melia—all, excited by the call to come and loot, rushed to the palace.

In a tearing hurry, the hungry ones robbed the store of delicious food and swallowed it. Some swooped on baskets of grains and carried them away. Many were just arriving there. Some were unfastening the gem-studded bracelets and waist-belts of girls and taking them away. The elephants were moving back and forth. Some, burning with lust, were rushing into the crowd and holding beautiful women in deep embrace. Some, fully intoxicated, were washing their mouths smeared with molasses. Some were distributing bundles of wealth among the people. There were some who were cutting open the bundles stacked in the storehouse with scissors. Some were enjoying bites of sweetmeats made of cheese. Some, entering the stable, were picking their choicest horses and riding away on them. Many, unable to manage the animals, fell off them and were rolling over the ground. Some were entering from the backyard and going out through the backdoor. Some, while pushing through the crowd, hit some mighty people and were treated with blows from them in return.

Most of things of the storehouse were taken away. What were they? Those were silk clothes designed for women, *gauri* cane, white *chamaras*, *chintamani* gem, ruby, *padmaraga* sapphire, *brahmajati* diamond, gold necklaces, flags, swords, bracelets, coral lamps, pearls collected from elephants' heads, *meshalorhana* emerald, earrings, *kusha mridanga*, Kashmiri crystal, white goose, gem lamps, *rudrajati* coral, ugala emerald, *indranila* sapphire, *jara mahura*, gold bracelets, armour, gem-studded gold articles, oyster with pearls, right-facing conch, *salagram*, *nagesvar* arrows, expensive clothes, *amrita* earrings, musk, oil, *panira nira*, *patabali* parrot, *bajratala* sheep, *kapila* cow, dancing monkey, *ratimuta* camel, white cuckoo, *bentakara* heron, single-ridged *rudraksha*, *pensiora* deer, *sindhujata* horse, *chandrajyoti* white elephants, *tabari taranga*, *suryaprabha* gem, *chandramandala* emerald, *paraveda* pearl, *rasathopa* pearl, Nepalese copper, brass, magnetic stone, horses of best breed, perfumes and aconite. After the rush melted away, the king adorned the throne and normalcy was restored. Some of the stolen commodities returned to the storehouse.

It was time of great rejoicing in the palace. The women of the palace treated the newborn baby with welcome rituals. For the protection of the baby they worshipped Goddess Sasthi with deep devotion. They named him Rudra Sudhanidhi. When he felt hungry he would cry in a voice as sweet as that of a cuckoo. Usually babies made the sound *kuhukuhu* when they cried, but in case of that baby it was '*shivoham! sarbagataham! santoham! suddhoham! nirbiroham! puryoham! kebalaham! sukshmoham! nityaham! nibidoham! chidanadoham! purusoham! puratanoham! chinmayoham! atmaham!*' Trapped by Vishnu's *maya*, he was subject to the three conditions of mind: the conscious, subconscious and unconscious. In spite of it he was concentrating on the soul as he cried. That's why he uttered the words '*shivoham! shivoham!*' whereas others said '*koham! koham!*' All those who heard him thought some evil power had cast a spell on him, and, to ward it off, they performed religious rituals.

The welcome ceremony was followed by feeding the baby with milk. As he put his mouth to his mother's breast, Goddess Mahamaya said to herself, 'This baby did not lose his consciousness when he was born. His cry seemed like delivering a set of advice. Vishnu's *maya* had no effect on him at all. When he grows up, he will never indulge in worldly affairs. His past virtues called *prarabdha* will soon bear fruit. He will dedicate himself entirely to *yoga*.' But for his ego, that he was a wise one, the Vaishnavi spread her *maya* on him as punishment. The *maya* found its way into him with the milk of her mother, which was first felt by the tongue. The more he took, the more he longed for it. He was soon occupied by ignorance. His meditation turned to a state of dream. As the dark cloud covers the moon, his wisdom became overshadowed by ignorance. His intellect, his realisation of God dissipated, making way for illusion, fear and loss of memory. Mahamaya's *maya* started first affecting the mouth which felt greedy for food. That was how he gambled away his wisdom and fell into the mire of ignorance.

As days went by, Rudra Sudhanidhi grew up like the moon after the new moon day. His appearance enchanted the elders; he looked like a white goose playing in a lotus forest. Five years elapsed. His body looked as radiant as gold melted five times. His face looked like the full moon, nose as long as a sesame flower and forehead as bright as the rising sun. His eyebrows looked like the black bees swarming around the lotus flower, his earrings like Jupiter and Venus, hung over his cheeks. His lips were looking like *malati* flower and hair blacker than collyrium. His eyes looked as enchanting as Madana's which charmed beautiful women. His body was as beautiful as *sirisa* flower, his throat like *jambura*, voice as solemn and clear as *dundubhi*, hands hanging from his chest over his thighs, gait like that of a young bull, nature as aggressive as a lion cub, body as radiant as the sun, finger nails like *jai* flowers, walk like that of a wild elephant and the soles of his feet like red lotuses, bearing the signs of fish and lotus. As a Shaivite *yogi*, who lost his way, he had all the attributes of a Vaishnava in addition. His astrological signs predicted that he was destined to be a Chakravarti and rule over the land and the sea.

To groom his son with proper education for a prosperous future, King Ananga Padmakar held a *puja* in honour of Lord Ganesha and Goddess Sarasvati with pomp and ceremony. He entrusted Pandit Udayan Acharya, a scholar of eminence with Brahma's blessings, with the task of teaching his son. After learning alphabets and arithmetic, Rudra Sudhanidhi switched over to the study of the eighteen parts of grammar. It included texts such as *Vyakarana Mahabhasya*, said to be originated from Shesanaga, *Panini Vyakarana*, evolving from Lord Shiva's *damaru*, *Chandramasa*, authored by Lord Chandra, *Sarasvata* by Goddess Sarasvati, *Ainda* and *Shruti Sagar*, written by Brihaspati and *Mahesvari* by Brahma. Besides, he read texts such as *Shakatayana*, *Aunadika*, *Sampadasika*, *Kalapa* and *Bardhaman*. The subtexts included *Anupama*, *Rasabata*, *Jumara* and *Akshata Kaumudi Chandrika*. Which portions of grammar did he learn? Those were alphabets, definitions, combining vowels and consonants, synonyms, substitution, rhyme, phonology, gender, person, number and verbal element.

Next he learnt shastras. Which *shastras*? Those were Mimamsa, Patanjala, Vaishesika, Kaumaraka, Pancharatra, Tarka and Agama. He went through the four Vedas and the Upanishads. He read *smruti shastras* authored by Manu, Yajnavalkya, Samkha and Brihaspati. For the benefit of the demons Narayan had some texts written by Brihaspati, to be taught by Shukracharya. He also studied Buddhist literature and the theories propounded by Kapalika, Kshapanika and Charvaka. Thereafter, he went through the eighteen Puranas. What were those? Those were *Matsya Purana, Kurma Purana, Varaha Purana, Bamana Purana, Bhavisya Purana, Markandeya Purana, Vishnu Purana, Nrusimha Purana, Agni Purana, Padma Purana, Itihasa Purana, Brahmanda Purana, Devi Purana, Shiva Purana, Bhagavata*, etcetera. It was followed by the study of Upapuranas. Then, he learnt the Jyotisa-shastra which contained the knowledge of days, the movement of the moon around the earth, *nakshatra*, conjunction of the moon, planetary positions, horoscopes, the auspicious time for journey and prediction of lifetime. Then, he read epics of all kinds such as *Kadambari*, *Naisadha*, *Rama-Charita*, *Bharata*, *Yogarnava Gita* and *Vasistha Ramayana*.

Which *Gita* did he read? He read *Bhagavata Gita, Bharata Gita, Pandava Gita, Uttara Gita, Yama Gita, Uddhava Gita, Abadhuta Gita, Ganga Gita, Yajnavalkya Gita, Parvati Gita, Maitreya Gita, Madalasa Gita, Kapota Gita, Kanaka Gita, Bhavisya Gita, Shiva Gita, Jada Gita, Ananda Gita, Shuka Gita, Pankaja Gita, Bhikshu Gita, Bhishma Gita* and *Brahma Gita*. It was followed by the study of Agamashastras and Rhetoric. Then, he studied books on acting by Bharata, composition of poetry, language, horses, elephants, treatment of diseases, palmistry, chariot-making, handicraft and art. Thus, he was well-versed in all *shastras*. He admired those who were virtuous and worthy of praise. He became a devotee of Vasudeva. He was trustworthy, generous and a lover of food.

This way ten years passed. The king engaged another teacher, Gunakar Acharya, to teach Dhanurveda to his son. That Acharya had mastered the subject by the grace of Lord Shiva. But Narayan Das had forgotten everything he had learnt by serving Lord Jagannatha and the Vaishnavas. Acharya taught the boy the sixty-four skills in archery—and how to use various weapons, such as *narayanastra*, *bajrastra*, *pashupatastra*, *ascharayastra*, *vrahmastra*, *chandrastra*, *barunastra*, *mahakalastra*, *rudrastra*, *agneyastra*, *meghastra*, *pavanastra*, *suryastra*, *mohanastra*, *indrastra*, *gandharvastra*, *kinnarastra*, *parvatastra*, *jalasosakastra*, *bayabastra*, *kuberastra*, *yamastra*, *amogha shakti*, *nagapasa*, and *jalapasa*. Through regular practice, Rudra Sudhanidhi made himself invulnerable.

At twelve, the prince became an adolescent. The hair on his body looked darker. His face reflected the signs of dislike for materialism. His body showed all the symptoms of a *yogi*. The one looking like Kandarpa now decked himself in a loin-cloth. The rows of teeth shone like the moon beam. His eyes became brighter; they looked like two black bees sitting on two lotus leaves in early winter. Seeing him, the king was struck by a sudden thought. He asked his minister, Bibeka Ratnakar, to find an auspicious day and go in search of a bride for his son. The minister circled around him three times and then, lay prostrate before him. Rising to his feet, he said with folded hands, 'Your Majesty! Most people sow seeds when it is time for harvest. It's of no use to sink a well when the house is on fire. O Lord! I have been looking for a bride since long, but could not find a suitable one in the Jambu Island. The messengers I had sent in the four directions have returned. Let's hear from them what information they have to offer.'

The king was sitting on the royal bed that looked like a sea of autumn cloud, the cover laid on it like a spread of foam. Surrounded by his courtiers, he looked like the moon among the stars. Looking like the moon beam, one thousand beautiful women, decked in finery, were fanning him. Their bangles tinkled as they fanned. It was then that the minister presented before him the four messengers who were sent in four directions.

First came the one, Sarbajana by name, who had been to the east. He had the rare ability to enter any place, no matter how impenetrable that place might be. He could see what was invisible to others. For his steadfast devotion to Lord Ganesha, he was blessed with those boons. He was proficient in astrology and could predict one's future. The all-knowing messenger fell at the king's feet, and, invoking Sarasvati, said, 'Your Majesty! As instructed by the minister, I visited all the kingdoms, but didn't find a suitable bride. I went to Bhata, Bhota, Malaba, Saurastra, Maharastra, Madhya Desa, Malana, Mandala, Sweta Parbata, Jhadamandala, Indraprastha, Hastina, Baruna, Jainta, Abanti, Ayodhya, Mathura, Gaya, Kashi, Kanchi, Mekhala, Meru, Maruta, Usma Desha, Antarvedi and Paduka. I went as far as Shiva Mandala along the east coast of the sea. I came across three maidens worthy of consideration. One was the daughter of the king of Kashi, located on the banks of the Jambubati River, next to the Manibanta Mountain. Her name was Anangabala; she was an epitome of virtues. Fair in complexion, she had eyes like those of a doe, breasts like *chakravaka*, gait like that of an elephant and voice like cuckoo's. Her waist was shaped like a *damaru*, her thighs thick and soft, hips like the seat of Kandarpa, teeth like the moon beam peeping through the clouds and her body like a flash of lightning in a cloud-swept sky. She had all the attributes worthy of praise, but the only defect in her was that the tip of her hair was brown. Another bride I saw in Bhadrasana kingdom, on the banks of the Mandakini. She was King Birabhadra's daughter, Lilavati by name. Her face was like the autumn moon, hair as black as darkness, eyes enchanting, eyebrows like a swarm of honey bees around lotus flowers and arms like lotus stems. She was of Padmini category. She had large hips and the kind of beauty that would seduce Kandarpa. The only demerit she had was that her teeth were protruding. I saw another bride in Natikal forest kingdom on the eastern coast located by the Chitra Tarangini River, near the shrine of Bhusandesvar Linga. She was the daughter of Chandraketu, king of Hiranyagarva. Her name was Manmathakala. Her face bloomed like a lotus flower; body of gold complexion and eyebrows looked like Kandarpa's bow. She had everything that a bride needed to have. But she lacked one thing; she had no mole sign on her face.'

Next came the messenger from the north. He said, 'Your Majesty! I travelled far into the north and visited all kingdoms there. With the magical gem on my ear that made the water solidify and some light food tucked to my waist, I walked on the sea. To me, the sea seemed to be made of glass. Then, putting on the magical shoes, I went farther and farther, visiting the islands that came my way. I saw an island of golden sand on which gems lay scattered. In some other island, there were platforms made of pearl, on which sages were found sitting in *samadhi-yoga*. Not fruits, but beds, jewellery and eatables grew on the trees there. Some islands were full of snakes. Somewhere else there were women with horse heads. I went as far as my eyes could see, but didn't find a bride to our choice.'

Thereafter the messenger from the west presented himself. Gunanidhana by name, he was a brahmin by caste and equal to Brihaspati in wisdom. He was well-versed in *mantras* and could achieve the impossible by performing yajnas. He said, 'Your Majesty! I went far into the west, but could not find a bride who would match the prince. I visited kingdoms such as Sindhu, Magadha, Maagadha, Mugala, Saindhaba Patana, Bhima Patana, Chitra Patana, Chitra Mandala, Chita Kutachala, mountains like Vindhya and Mandara, rivers and the sea. I met King Bairipannaga of Madhuvati kingdom, by the Amritkal River. As rich as Kubera, he had Mukutavati as his chief queen. They had a daughter named Madanaballava who possessed all the virtues. Her face was so beautiful as if seen through Kandarpa's mirror. So was her smile. Her eyes, extended to her ears and looked like blue water-lilies. The front layer of her eyes was as white as hundreds of Milky Sea, the autumn lilies, *kunda* flowers, Vishnu's conch, a sword made of pearl, the waves of the Mandakini and foam and froth of the ocean from which Lakshmi had emerged. Her pupils were as beautiful as blue emerald, the new monsoon cloud, blue water-lilies, peacock's neck and flowers without petals. Her lips were as red as pomegranate flower, *malati* flower, ripe *bimba* fruit, red water-lily, red lotus, ruby, the rising sun and hibiscus flower. The only point of objection was that she had no signs of conch, lotus, flag, goad and wheel on her.

I came across a mountain of gems in a land in the western province. Its radiance made the sun look like a glow worm. There was a big banyan tree there, the branches of which were made of gold. It had three branches; they were too dazzling to look at. Under it, there stood a mound of gems which looked as bright as the sun. Down the mound, I saw a man sitting. He was white in complexion and looked as radiant as thousands of rising moon. A seven-hooded snake had coiled up around his head.

He had put on a deep blue cloth around his waist. He had a rainbow coloured garland hanging from his neck. His eyes looked like the moon. The snake had a jewel on each of its hoods, the light of which rose like flames that touched the sky. He had a wish-fulfilling *chintamani* necklace around his neck. The enormous effect of the necklace had enlightened the fellow *siddhas* and had made the land prosperous by the blessings of Lakshmi. The venom that the snake spat out had caused the Ganga shrink in size. Using the *mantras* I was blessed with, I reached the foot of the mountain. I found women of divine origin loitering there. I also saw moon-like lotuses blooming in a pond filled with nectar-like water. The philaments of the flowers were of golden colour which looked like *padmaraga* gem. Their fragrance was wafted away by the wind over a distance of one hundred *yojanas*. The colour of the lotuses seemed to have covered the moon with red clouds in the evening. Lakshmi used to visit the pond for relaxation. A woman of Padmini category used to emerge from each flower. All of them had lotus-faces, lotus-eyes, lotus-smell and lotus-hands and feet. In the morning they were born as babies;

they appeared as young women at midday, turned to old women in the evening and disappeared at night. Had they been young throughout the day they would have been a nice match for our prince. Then, I advanced further. I covered the mountains such as Bhudas, Debadas and Purusadas. But I didn't find a suitable bride.' This said, he drew aside, his head in his hands.

Then appeared the messenger who had been to the south. He was Baichitra by name. He was smart; he had mastered Chintamani Vidya, by virtue of which he could fetch things, unheard of and unseen. He had access to every place and was able to remove the obstacles that came his way. He bowed to the king, and, with folded hands, said, 'Your Majesty! I went in south direction. I travelled across Banga, Kalinga, Telanga, Sourastra, Maharastra, Bichinta, Mahachinta, Khamandala, Chaurya Mandala, Jala Mandala, Chedi Mandala, Kanchi Marua, Paya, Panchavartara, many islands, mountains such as Mahindra, Mahendra, Malaya, Mahendra Tanaya and rivers such as the Godavari, the Krishnaveni and the Kaveri. Nowhere did I find a bride of our choice.'

Last but not least, the messenger from the north arrived. His name was Shashadha. He said, 'Your Majesty! By the blessings of the Divine mother I possess some rare qualities. Visiting the kingdoms in the north, one after another, I reached Haridwar by which the Mandakini flows in three streams from an elephant's teeth. After passing many mountains of divine look, I took the path called Pandava Marg. In fact, the Divine Mother carried me on her shoulder and took me to a mountain that lies next to the Himachal. When looked at closely, one can see the reflection of all the worlds on it. As it happened to a moon-stone when kept in moonlight, the mountain produced beads of nectar flowing from its summit. Its radiance illumined heaven. The Milky Sea surrounded it on four sides while the Ganga fell from its top. It seemed as if a white elephant had entered a sea of nectar. The sun and the moon hung from the sky on both sides like a pair of clocks. The stars appeared as flowers strewn on the elephant. The clouds of vibrant colours looked like decorations of the elephant. The crimson colour of the sunset in the western sky looked like a mark of vermilion on the elephant's forehead. The waters of the Ganga cascading down on the emerald peak looked like a rain of strong, scented juice exuded from the temples of the elephant in rut. The rumbling of the white clouds seemed like the trumpeting of the elephant. Its two eyes looked like Mercury and Venus planets. There, in the mountain was a lake called Manasarovara. The Moon God used to emerge out of it and disappear into the nether world through it.

The Ganga, looking like the moon, flowed into it. One who bathed in it, received God's blessings. There was a bull on its banks who was of golden complexion. Its horns looked like gems. It was as mighty as a lion and as radiant as the rising sun. Its reflection on the mountain looked like two insects on the two sides of the elephant. The eyes of the bull looked like emerald. That bull was sleeping, bending its head over its back. A man sat near it, leaning his back against it. Looking radiant, that man was so white in complexion that it seemed as if the whiteness of his body had pervaded the whole world. He had long, matted hair, as wavy as the waters of the Kalandi and was looking like black snakes hanging from his head. It seemed as if the elephant was tethered with ropes of black *pata* silk. A cascade of water, as white as the moonbeam was tumbling down on it with a great noise, and then, flowing out with a murmuring sound. There was a crescent moon on his head without stain which illumined the mountain. The demi-gods frolicking there felt as if they were in heaven. The great snakes were living on the light of the moon. Some of those looked like molten gold, some like roaring fire, some like the sun, some like gems, some like rainbow, some like the philaments of lotus. They were playing merrily in his matted hair and the gems on their hoods, thousands in number, emitted their light that seemed as if there was a rain of fire from the sky.

That man's blue eyebrows were like the wish-fulfilling Kamadhenu cow or like the black marks on the moon made into an arch. He had three eyes: the right one the sun, the left one the moon and the third one on his forehead was like a huge ball of fire. When looked closely, they seemed to reflect the three worlds. One could hardly stare at them. He was clad in a piece of tiger skin; his throat was blue like that of a peacock or the cloud or the Jambu river. That was why he was called Nilakantha, one with a blue throat. His legs were like lotus stems and arms swelling with muscles. He had four hands, each like a five-hooded snake and finger-nails like gems on their hoods. His earrings were glittering like sun rays which seemed to reach the Pole Star. One of the snakes, as fierce as fire, served as his sacred thread. In his upper hands he was holding a trident and a *damaru* while the lower ones were in a blessing posture. He was meditating in *samadhi-yoga* and was as still as a mountain.

Beside him, there stood another man looking like king of death who would destroy the three worlds. Brown in complexion and as radiant as the sun, he had the face of a monkey. He held a trident in his hand; he was giving protection to the mountain. To his right was a boy with the face of an elephant busy playing with the Basuki cobra. At a distance, lay a golden mouse. In front of the man in meditation stood a woman who had the beauty of crores of Kandarpa which Kamadeva, Shesanaga and Sarasvati could hardly describe. Crores of Lakshmi were emerging from her lotus-feet. She had three eyes, shaped like lotuses, which looked like mirrors to see the three worlds, one of which was the earth. She bore a smile on her face. The charm of her sidelong look could hardly be felt through human intellect. One who watched her, ages would appear to him as a moment. The man in *samadhi* had fixed his gaze on her face. One of her eyes, which was the sun, was in a state of *yoga*, while the eye representing fire roved over the earth. Had not she had three eyes, had she been someone other than Parvati, she would have been the best choice for the prince. Bowing to the man in meditation, the Divine Mother brought me back to your place!'

Hearing the words of the messengers, the king broke down in grief. The thought that there was no bride for his son on the earth kept haunting him.

CHAPTER 4

Kamananda Yogi: Tailokya Bijaya

A few days later a *yogi* named Kamananda arrived there. He seemed to be a wonderful man. As handsome as Kandarpa, he was in his early youth. His appearance was as impressive as that of a lion in its adolescence. His gait was like that of a wild elephant. He could easily enchant young women. His face was like the moon and rings on his ears were beautiful. As a king had his courtiers around him, he was surrounded by ghosts, *betalas*, *yakshinis* and Matruka Chandi, who were not visible to public eye. He had mastered the skills of *yoga*; his vision encompassed the three worlds. He was well-versed in the manual of Vedic rites, known as *kalpa* which included Nimakalpa, Gandhakalpa, Nagakalpa, Rasakalpa Abhrakalpa, Karpurakalpa, Nirgundikalpa, Manikalpa, Rodantikalpa, Kshirakalpa and Dhatrikalpa. He was also familiar with the *Kalpachintamani*, the *Garuda Purana*, the *Kautukachintamani* and Buddhist literature.

He had achieved excellence in the yogic practice called Mani Sadhana. How many types of Mani? Those were Jalastambhana Mani, Agni Stambhana Mani, Rasa Stambhana Mani, Subarnakarana Mani, Mohanakarana Mani, Ulluka Mani, Kuhuka Mani, Khechara Mani, Kamagrahana Mani, Amrita Mani, Akata Mani, Urddhagati Mani, Sarbadasi Mani, Patala Mani, Nidhipravesa Mani, Drustadrusta Mani, Dipa Mani, Manduka Mani, Naga Mani, Shosana Mani, Mohana Mani, and Divya Mani. With the help of a text titled *Tantra Chudamani*, he accomplished the most impossible tasks. The modes of meditation he adopted included Kalpataru Sadhana, Chintamani

Sadhana, Panchubaktra Sadhana, Garuda Rudra Sadhana, Chaturbhuja Sadhana, and Kamadhenu Sadhana.

Putting on a red cloth, he worshipped skulls in the cremation ground to tame the eight *betalas*. He performed the ritual of pouring the blood of a black sheep into the ember of a dead body already cremated and brought all the evil spirits under his control. Sitting on a dead body, facing east, under a banyan tree on the banks a river at dead of night, he invoked Chandi, reading out *mantras*. Then, he propitiated the sixty-four *yoginis*. With austerity, he worshipped Matruka Shiva, a *yogini*, reciting a twelve-lettered *mantra*. He invoked Yogini Bharija with an eight-lettered *mantra*. It took seven days for him to harness Yogini Ratipriya. Accompanied by one thousand attendants, she used to seduce men, fulfil their wishes and bless them with exquisite houses, dainty dishes and gold. She took delight in having unlimited sex and liked to share the bed with a man as a wife did. He pleased Karnapisachi with *kanchana* flowers, smearing her body with ghee and offering her porridge made from *apamarga* rice and milk of a single-coloured cow in a skull-pot. She could tell the news of the places within a radius of one hundred *yojanas*. He pleased another *yogini*, Sarbamanoharini by praying to her in the Mandarabana on the banks of the Mandakini, reciting a *mantra* of eleven letters. She had the rare quality of influencing the minds of the gods, *gandharvas*, *yakshas*, *kinnaras*, human beings and ghosts. Next he invoked Yakshini Kamalini by placing her on an eight-petalled lotus near a pond of lotuses, offering her a lotus garland and reciting a *mantra* of eight letters for eight days. She had the power to offer a lot of wealth to her devotees. Likewise he prevailed on Yakshini Upasarpa by performing fire rituals, burning *bahada* wood and offering her blue blackberries and blue lotus and reading out a twelve-lettered *mantra*. She could present chariots, horses, elephants, foot-soldiers, thrones and many other wonderful things with great interest. This way he prevailed on the sixty-four *yoginis*, including Bharija, Matruka, Karnapisachi,

Sarbamanoharini, Kamalini, Upasarpa, Darsani, Betalamohini, Jalandhari, Birupakshi, Siddhamata, Bhagni and Surasundari and achieved the ability to create miracles.

Performing *tantrika* rituals, he had cast a spell on Brahma Kumar Chanda, Maguni Chanda, Utsistha Chanda and Chiranjibi Chanda, each with a stick in hand, who could read the minds of others and entertain them with their antics. Performing due rituals, both Vedic and *tantrika*, he had won the favour of goddesses such as Tripura, Tripurasundari and Bhubanesvari. Reciting the one-lettered *mantra* and offering animal sacrifices, he had pleased Bhubanesvari who commanded the six *chakra*s and her followers such as Lakini, Kakini, Hakini, Dakini and Bakini. Adorned with a crown of crescent moon, she appeared before him and said, 'Kamananda! I will fulfil your wishes'. Lying prostrate before her, the *yogi* begged her with folded hands, 'Your kind words make me feel as if drinking nectar'. When the Goddess told him to ask for a boon, he replied, 'Grant me what you consider the best for a human'. The Goddess explained, 'The best thing for a man is to aspire for salvation which is not within my jurisdiction. None other than Srikrishna can grant it. I would advise you to try for it'. 'What is salvation?' the *yogi* asked. The Goddess replied, 'It is that state of mind in which there is no contact, no action, no intellect, no ego, no consciousness, no dreaming-only the being, a condition of deep joyful experience, beyond consciousness. It is the symbol of Truth, Eternity and Immortality. It is the Ultimate Reality that exists for all eternity.' The *yogi* asked, 'Is there any room for worldly enjoyment in salvation? Can one have delicious food to eat? Can one make love to beautiful women? Can one possess divine powers? Can he have things that are rare?'

Hearing this, the Goddess answered, 'The world you are looking for is another hell which gives no consideration to wisdom. In salvation there is no speaker, nor speech, nor listener, nor seer, nor philosophy-nothing. So, the question of entertaining ignorance and delusion does not arise.' The *yogi* quipped, 'I have nothing to do with salvation, then. How can there be joy without worldly attachment? Sensual pleasure is the real happiness and the real wisdom. Look at Lord Shiva who bears the moon on his head! Half of his body is shared by Himalaya's daughter. He derives pleasure out of it. That he says women are distractions is just a ploy to befool the world. Going without food, exposing oneself to sun and winter, sans friends, dwelling in the forest—can there be joy in any of these? Happiness lies in living in a grand mansion, embracing beautiful women in a moonlit night, their bodies smeared with sandalwood paste, listening to the *veena* while a gentle breeze blows in the garden of flowers. There can be no wisdom without attachment, senses and intellect. O Mother! If you like to grant me a boon, kindly listen to what I wish for. May this body of mine be young and healthy ever. May my involvement in the pleasures of the flesh not affect me adversely. May it not be regarded as a sin if I sleep with a thousand women. May the food I eat be digested. May I go wherever I wish to. May I get everything I wish to have. May not fire burn me. May my handsomeness enchant all . Fulfil all my wishes, if you so like.' As he finished, the Goddess burst into laughter and told him, 'My son! You ask for a life of sensual pleasures. For this, you will have to follow those instructions which I had heard from Lord Shiva long ago, sitting in his lap on a crystal platform. Now listen to me carefully.

Awake before sunrise. Wash your bowel thoroughly. The wash is of many kinds: Chandra Surya *pakhala*, Nagarjuna *pakhala*, Jalapuraka *pakhala*, Ghatika Srabana *pakhala*, Trigundi *pakhala*, Malabhanda *pakhala* and Navichakra *pakhala*. Thereafter smear your body with cold ash and take the *kalpamahausadhi*. Thinking on the Sun God, sit in a yogic posture called *asana*. *Asana-yoga* is of eighty-four kinds. Some of these are *siddhasana*, *Kumudasana*, *kamalasana*, *vajrasana*, *virasana*, *sukhasana*, *chibukasana*, *chakrasana*, *sirsasana*, *parbasana*, *dhanurasana*, *kulasana*, *bhekasana*, *kamathasana*, *bhadrasana* and *svastikasana*. Of the eighty-four *asana*s four are of great significance. These are *padmasana*, *bhadrasana*, *svastikasana* and *siddhasana*. First sit in *siddhasana* pose. How is it? Press the tip of your left foot tightly against your thigh. Then, put your right foot on your genitals. Remain steady. Your throat, chest and navel should be in a vertical line. Don't raise or lower your body too much. Sit tight. Keep your hands in control. Touch your chin to your chest. Press your belly with both hands. Fix your eyes on the tip of your nose. Meditate on the *apana* air at the navel. Hold *prana* air in your heart. This is called *sadhana-yoga*. Besides, there are eighteen postures of which Matta Matanga Keshari, Odiani and Jalandhari are more important. Again, there are sixty-four hand postures, some of which are Udaya, Ullasa, Khechari, Gagana, Parama, Sankhini, Sambhavi, Bhairavi, Amruta, Kapali, Mulamukha, Olata, Bikata, Mahadrasta, Tanaya, Talaya, Bhubi, Ardha and Urddha. Of these, the most important ones are Khechari, Sambhavi, Amruta and Bhuvi. Twist the tip of your tongue to brush against the palate, take Sambhavi posture, considering your whole body to be the fourteen worlds. Imagine that the lower part of your body from the sole of your feet to the thigh as the nether world. Imagine the soles of your feet as Rasatala, the feet as Mahatala, legs as Talatala, ankles as Sutala, the gap behind the knee-joint as Vitala, the knee as Atala and thighs as Patala. There are six esoteric points in the body called *chakra*s (energy centres), the topmost one located in the crown of the head and represented by a lotus with one thousand petals. The central post called *meru danda* lies to its left which is divided into sixteen parts, each part called a *damaru*. Some of these are *vayu damaru*, *agni damaru*, *surya damaru*, *brahma damaru* and *deva damaru*. *Brahma damaru* is the gateway to Brahma's abode, *rudra damaru* to Shiva's, *bhairava damaru* makes one immortal, *kala damaru* makes one outlive time, *kama damaru* fulfils one's sex desires and *urdha damaru* is the gateway to heaven.

Each *damaru* has a presiding deity of its own. For example, *brahma damaru* is presided by Brahma, *rudra damaru* by Rudra and *bhairava damaru* by Kala. The *damarus* also represent the sixteen parts of the moon, such as Aloka, Kallolini, Ujjalanti, Unmadimi, Karangini, Somayanti, Lambata, Lahari, Lola, Lalati, Prakruti, Sribanti, Pravahi, Sannadha, Prasanni and Prasadusila. These *damarus* constitute the Meru of which the human body is made. The Meru has twelve peaks called twelve *nadis* which are energy channels. They are named as *ida*, *pingala*, *sushumna*, *gandhari*, *hastijihva*, *pusa*, *alambusa*, *kaukshi*, *sankhini* and *svastata*. *Ida* and *pingala* originate from the nostrils. *Sushumna* extends to *brahmarandhra*, *hastijihva* originates from the lips, *gandhari* from the ears, *pusa* and *alambusa* from the eyes, *kaukshi* from the anus, *sankhini* from the genitals and *svastata* proceeds to the *brahmarandhra*, *ida* is white in colour, *pingala* yellow, *sushumna* the colour of the flame, *gandhari* blue, *pusa* red, *alambusa* colour of the smoke, *kaukshi* brown, *hastijihva* green and *sankhini* white. There is a total of seventy-two thousand *nadis* which are different from each other in structure and function.

After *asana*, comes *pranayama*. Start it by reciting *om* which is called *pranava*. Take the air through the left nostril and stock it in the lotus at the navel. Think on Narayan and pass the air back through the right nostril. Take air through *ida* and leave it through *pingala*. Repeat the process. It is called light *pranayama*. The next phase is withdrawal. After breathing exercises take a little food. You have to give up the food which is bitter or salty or sour or astringent or sweet in taste, as they activate the *rajas* and *tamas*. As substitute, you may, however, take *bimba* fruit for bitter, *haridra* for astringent, *amla* for sour, honey for sweet, ginger for pungent and black salt for salty. As the main course, you may take sugar cane juice, cow-milk oats, saliana rice, jaggery, black pepper, parbal, coconut and *krushnataila* cooking oil. Fill half of your belly with food, leave a quarter of it for water and another quarter for air. This dieting is called *pratyahara* or withdrawal.

Next comes meditation. Meditation is of many kinds: *sunythula, patalakasha, ardha, urddha, mandhya, nadi chakra, prana pabana, jyoti prakash, gagana satadala, kundalini, prativa, nibida, andhakara, abyakula, basana, abayaba* and *panchabhuta.* Feel the presence of the gods and goddesses inside your body: Lord Indra in the hands, Vishnu in the feet, the Wind God in your gait, Fire God in the navel, Lord Yama in the stomach, the Moon God in the mind, Lord Kala in the tongue, Goddess Kalaratri in your sleep, Narayan in the face and Sky God in the ears. Meditate on them with steadfast loyalty.

The act of concentrating the mind on the object of meditation is called *dharana.* There are sixty-four types of *dharana,* some of which are Birama, Sahasrachakra, Badabanala, Parvati, Panchabhuta, Paramahamsa, Himavanta, Diggaja, Sarasvati and Mahesvar. The *yogi*s who do it outlive the deluge. By practising Bajrakila *dharana,* the period between the creation and the deluge appear as a moment. One can do it by Jagannatha's blessings. Bhusandakaka Barana and Parvati *dharana*s keep a *yogi* safe from the destructive effects of the deluge. Those who have done all the sixty-four *dharana*s are Balabhadra and Hanuman. Nandikesvar knows ten *dharana*s, Kartikesvar ten, Shiva's bull twelve, Lord Shiva all the sixty-four, Mahakala twenty-two, Bisvakeshan twenty-one and Jaya and Bijaya twenty-seven. Those whom Jagannatha blesses can do four times sixty-four *dharana.* This is called *dharana-yoga.* Finally some *dharana*s culminate in a state of *samadhi.* It makes a man immortal. Great *mahatma*s only can accomplish it. Their patience is as unshakable as crores of mountains. They are as strong as crores of lions, as determined as crores of Lord Yama and their hearts as hard as crores of thunder. They are as sacred as crores of skies, as learned as crores of Brihaspati, as single-minded as crores of sages, as radiant as crores of sun, as full as crores of seas, as healthy as crores of Dhanvantari and as resourceful as crores of richmen. Lord Shiva and Balabhadra are the ones who possess all these attributes. Those who are as lustful as horses, who are habitual liers and who take to excessive drinking have no control over their senses. Devilsh in nature, they are prone to many diseases. They cannot enter the world of Yoga unless Jagannatha is kind to them. Narayan Das, taking the dust from the feet of Jagannatha's servitors, has been able to know it.'

In obedience to the instructions of Goddess Bhubanesvari, Kamananda engaged himself in yogic practices, by virtue of which he could have an appearance similar to Kandarpa's. By worshipping Kamakshi, he gained the knowledge of hypnotism. He attained *siddhi* in most matters. He could move mountains, force his enemies concede defeat and go anywhere he liked. All his achievements were limited to his intellect only as he was not devoted to Vasudeva. This Yoga was first narrated by God to Sarasvati who passed it on to Bhubanesvari. Taking pity on Kamananda, Bhubanesvari told Kamananda about it. Narayan Das knew it by serving at Srikrishna's feet.

Here the fourth chapter, titled 'Tailokya Bijaya', comes to an end. The fifth part will be named 'The First Rain of Sudhanidhi'. Those who listen to it, prosper in life.

CHAPTER 5

The First Rain of Sudhanidhi

There was a ghost named Anila Khechara who was as swift as fire. Blue and grey in complexion, he had eyes as red as planet Mars. He could enter the sun's abode at will. Normally as tall as a palm tree, he could enlarge his body so as to touch the Pole Star, if he so wished. He could tell the past and the future. He regarded himself as a disciple of Lord Shiva. He could go to most hard-to-reach places, if he liked. He could withstand cyclones, blow horn with his mouth, devour hard substances, stay in water, fire and wind, call out to those in far-off places, bear with the strike of thunderbolt, fly in the sky, travel across the three worlds in a moment's time, disappear into the sky, make himself invisible or visible, cross the path of lightning, enchant women, devour the enemies, steal the wealth of others, take many forms and swim across the river.

He could carry a sword in his hand, move against the wind, fly like a bird and speak in human language. He was reduced to a ghost as his devotion to Vasudeva lacked sincerity. As he pleased Parvati by his dance, she took pity on him and protected him in times of deluge. She treated him as her own son. That ghost named Anila Khechara became one of Kamananda's companions. Kamananda had lured him into his fold with the help of his spiritual power. The ghost community was divided into many ranks, some fifth, some sixth and some seventh. Those between the eighth and twelfth rank were called Chanda, between the thirteenth and fifteenth rank *betala*, between the sixteenth and eighteenth Vidyadhara and between the nineteenth and twenty-one were called Kshudralinga. Those of the twenty-fourth rank were known as *siddhas*. In spite of possessing some divine qualities, Anila Khechara was turned to a ghost for his own fault. The ghosts were graded as *adhibhuta*, *mahabhuta* and *divyabhuta*. Lord Ganesha and Anil Khechara were *divyabhutas*.

Anila Khechara was ordained the commander of the army of ghosts, devils, *yakshinis*, *chandas* and *betalas*, which Kamananda had in his control. Parvati had conferred on him the title Bhuta Chudamani. One day Kamananda, patting him on the back, said, 'Leader of the ghosts! Didn't you tell me the other day that a rudra called Abhinaba Chaitanya was born in this city, bearing the name Rudra Sudhanidhi? You said he was well-versed in *shastras* and an epitome of virtues. He was an asset to his kingdom, but had no memory of his past birth. You also added that a girl named Abidya Mrutyusanjibani Karani had taken birth and that they were made for each other. Tell me, how and where she is now. That will please my ears. I want nothing else; I will feel like drinking nectar to hear about her. I will hold her in deep embrace. Enchanted by her urn-shaped breasts, I hope to cross the sea of lust. All the beauty of the three worlds is stored in her. I will make love to her and be happy forever. She may be a *vidyadhari* or a Goddess or a woman of the Naga clan or Daksha's daughter or Shiva's consort or a heavenly damsel or a well-built, doe-eyed woman. My friend! I can abduct any beautiful woman from anywhere in the three worlds, let alone her. Tell me where she is, about whose birth you had mentioned before.' Hearing this, the ghost replied, 'O great Yogi! Lord Shiva blessed her with an everlasting youth. Parvati told her, 'Go on meditating on the banks of the Manasarovara. After some days you will go to the earth with King Dharmadhvaja and live in his house as his daughter. In due course of time you will get your husband, who is equal to Lord Shiva.'

In obedience to her instructions, she left for the banks of the Manasarovara. Her face looked like the rising moon of the second day. There was a lotus forest in the Manasarovara where golden lotuses bloomed. Their philaments were made of ruby, cupola of diamond, stalk of emerald, stem of crystal and pollen grains of vermilion. Its honey was like nectar. The mud on which they grew was made of musk. The light emanated from them rose in flames. Dews did not harm them. They bloomed at every moonrise and never faded. The Wind God never entered there, nor the honey bees ever sucked their honey.

Lakshmi Devi, accompanied by her maids, often came there for recreation. One day, while making merry with her attendants, her eyes fell on Abidya Mrutyusanjibani Karani. She stared at her with compassionate eyes. Surprised, she looked at her face again and again. She would look at herself and then, at her in wonder. She thought: God never tolerates anyone's pride. He has created this girl to teach a lesson to those who claim themselves to be the most beautiful ones. The maids were watching both of them alternately. To them both were looking equally beautiful. Bewildered, Lakshmi asked them, 'Do I look like this maiden?' They replied, 'O Goddess! You are Lakshmi, Narayan's chief consort. How can you be compared with others? She looks like your daughter. A daughter in her youth, of course, looks more enchanting than her mother.' Hearing this, Lakshmi mused, 'If Narayan happens to see this maiden, he will abandon me. Males are like bumble bees; they prefer to have the fresh ones. The best way to avoid it is to accept her as my daughter so that Narayan would never think of marrying his own daughter.' With this in mind, she called the maiden to come near her, and, decking her in finery, declared her as her daughter.

Adjacent to the Meru Mountain, on the seashore near Madhubela forest, there was a kingdom called Prithi Tilak, ruled by King Dharmadhvaja. His chief queen was Kokilabati by name. The king was a Vaishnava through and through. Righteous as he was, he had dedicated his body and soul to Vasudeva, completely oblivious of his external identity. He was as good as an inanimate object. His maids used to look after him. His eyes and ears were open, but he could neither see nor hear anything. To him heat and cold were alike. In such situation, his courtiers had to look after the affairs of the kingdom. He had lost the sense of taste; he could not say whether the food was bitter or astringent or sour or pungent or salty. The maids had to feed him with their hands. Leaving his personal and royal identity aside, he continued to be the king in name only. On the day of *ekadashi* he would spend a sleepless night meditating on Vishnu with the holy lamp on his head. One day the enemy forces launched an attack on his kingdom. When the messenger reached him to deliver the news, he found the king in a state of *samadhi*. At the time the king's mind was focused on the signs of fish, flag, goad, conch, lotus, wheel and *matsyarekha* on Vishnu's lotus-feet; he could hardly hear a word of what the messenger said. The king's army led by the courtiers failed to prevent the enemy forces from advancing. Taking advantage of it, the enemies laid siege to the kingdom and looted the houses. The queens sang and danced before him to break his silence, but it was all in vain. When the invasion force attempted to set the city on fire, the *sudarsan chakra* that Vishnu had deployed there to protect the Vaishnavas sprang into action. Thus the city could be saved. The king had no fascination for women and sex. He had given up all his earthy desires. That's why in spite of his inaction, the *sudarsan* wiped out all the enemies.

Queen Kokilabati was a devotee of Goddess Lakshmi. She used to pray to her with steadfast loyalty. Pleased with her devotion the Goddess appeared before her at midnight when she was in meditation. Her feet were not touching the ground. The Goddess was looking more radiant than thousands of moons, thousands of suns, thousands of lightnings, thousands of flames and thousands of gems—all taken together. Her radiance seemed to illumine the three worlds. Her sidelong looks would make the whole world melt and lose their senses. Those looks would even affect Kamadeva in the same way. That was the cause of Narayan taking his birth and Ananta carrying the earth on his head. That had motivated all the actions in the world. That look gave form to the formless *Brahman* and caused the birth of Brahma, Indra, Rudra and the eight Lakshmis. It seemed as if drops of nectar were falling from her eyes. Were the moon and the sun rising from the corners of her compassionate eyes? The beauty of all the moons that had existed since the creation began was far too inferior to the charm of her moon-like face, which words would fail to describe. Didn't Kamadeva, inspired by it, enchant the gods, for which he was called Devadalana? To impress Narayan she had a pair of earrings shaped as wheels—one the symbol of life and the other of knowledge. The gods, *gandharva*s, *yaksha*s and *kinnar*s were of the opinion that those earrings had held Kamadeva captive there. They shone like the rays of the sun. The pearl necklace around her conch-shaped throat looked like drops of nectar the gods bathed in. Her breasts seemed as if they were the storehouse of all the wealth of the world. The beads of sweat that speckled her body looked like the waters of the deluge. It seemed Kamadeva was lost in thought at the sight of her breasts. Her navel, looking like a deep hole, seemed to hide all the joys of the world. The folds at her waist looked like Narayan's fingers on the bow-string. Her feet symbolized the source of wisdom, wealth and glory that everyone pined for. Her feet had the complexion of the rising sun. The radiance of her finger-nails seemed to dispel the surrounding darkness.

Such was Lakshmi Devi, seated on a lotus, a white gem on her forehead, a garland around her neck, white lotus in her hands, decked in white clothes, white flowers tucked to her bun and her body smeared with white sandalwood paste. She was riding a chariot, decorated with white *chamara*s and drawn by four white horses. Four white elephants stood by her sides pouring sacred water on her head from four white pots. In such appearance Lakshmi Devi presented herself before Kokilabati. She told Kokilabati to ask for a boon. At the first sight, Kokilabati passed out. Her heart began to pound with joy. She could not decide whether she was a man or woman. She could not dare look at her face, the kind of which she had neither seen nor heard about before. Regaining her senses, she looked at her with the eyes of a woman and regarded her for a moment. With folded hands, she begged her, 'Mother! If you are so kind, bless me with a child who looks exactly like you'. With a smile on her lips the Goddess told her with consolatory words, 'There is one who is the spitting image of myself. Parvati had given birth to her as one of her incarnations. She is in human form. Pleased with your devotion, I am offering her to you.'

Saying so, she presented Abidya Mrutyusanjibani before her. Holding her hand, the Goddess told the queen, 'I had adopted her as my daughter. She means everything to me. Gauri had brought her up with love and care. She will marry a man of exceptional character. I put her in your charge. Look after her with greatest care. Treat her the same way you treat me. One day you will feel proud of her. She is not born from human womb; she is destined to marry someone imbibed with the characteristics of God. Don't marry her off against her will. She will choose her own man. Arrange a *svayamvar* for her, inviting many princes. If she refuses to marry anyone of them, send them back.' Handing over the maiden to the queen, she whispered into Abidya's ears, 'Look, dear! On the thirteenth day in the bright fortnight of Chaitra, a young man will meet you on the banks of Sveta Sarovara. He will look at you intently, describe your breasts as divine objects, put a gem necklace around your neck and compare your eyes with the crescent-shaped head ornament. Know that he is your man. You will see him in your dream shortly.' Instructing her thus and declaring her as the king's daughter, she hastened to Vaikuntha to serve at Vishnu's lotus-feet.

O great Yogi! The one you are looking for lives in king Dharmadhvaja and queen Kokilabati's palace in the Prithi Tilak kingdom. She has the power to enchant Brahma, Indra and Rudra, let alone the common men. She is too beautiful to be seduced by anyone. Besides, the kingdom is guarded by the *sudarshan chakra.* As you asked me to name the most beautiful woman of the world I told you all this. Now it's up to you to find ways to have her.' Hearing this, the *yogi* was erotically stimulated. Holding his friend in deep embrace, he begged him benignly, 'Fetch her to me somehow.' From then, he fell prey to Kamadeva.

His breath changed from cold to hot. He lost interest in food. He was at his wit's end. The moonlight appeared very hot to him. His cheerful face fell. He sweltered in the spring wind. He simmered in the heat of love. Any talk about the maiden delighted him. He sweated wet. All his thoughts turned to her. He felt as if she was with him. Wherever he looked, her image appeared before him. He found himself in a state of frenzy. He forgot *yoga*; his concentration of mind was disturbed. Love for the feminine element occupied his mind. His heartbeat quickened. Rotting in the mire of lust, his health was damaged. Unable to bear the pangs of separation, he told Anila Khechara, 'Dear friend! What use our staying here when the woman is there? Let's hurry to her place paying no heed to the wheel. We will abduct her anyhow. She is in no way more powerful than the *gandharva* and the *kinnara* women. Then, he examined the flow of wind through his nostrils, and, choosing an auspicious moment, he ordered the *betalas* to carry him to Prithi Tilak kingdom. Blowing the conch and with the help of his spiritual powers, he produced a chariot that looked like crystal. The flags hanging from it were like lightnings and its wheels were of smoke. The chariot looked like a cloud of mist and its sound was as deafening as that of thunder. One thousand female fiends were yoked to it.

What did they look like? Some had their heads bent low. Some had the heads of tiger, some of jackal, some of vulture, some of cat, some of crow, some of horse and some of cow. Thinking on Bhairava and smiling inwardly, Kamananda Yogi mounted the chariot. Surrounded by ghosts, he looked like Lord Shiva. The journey started. Leading from the front were the ghosts of the colour of smoke, looking like patches of cloud. Each of them had a cattle bone in his hand. Letting out a loud roar, they were moving in the sky. Sometimes they would swoop on the passers-by and demand juice and green coconut from them. They would drown someone in water and sweep away the washing *ghats*. They would also trouble the male children when they saw them. They were followed by the departed souls called *preta* who were as tall as thirteen hands. They had pointed faces and distended bellies. They were ever thirsty. As commanded by the *yogi*, the *chandas* were busy supplying water to them. Next were the male fiends circling each other, swinging like elephants and playing like monkeys. They grabbed whatever they found on their way. Behind them were the *betalas*, as huge as mountains, with iron sticks in their hands. Each of them was mightier than the other. The *chandas* were walking behind them. In the rearmost position were the sixty-four *yoginis* riding their carriers. Each of them had a *chamara* in her hand.

Anila Khechara, the commander of ghosts, was sitting on a caparisoned big horse. Some of the *betalas* were riding the horses whom they had got from the forest. They had their *yakshini* wives in their laps, roaring loudly. Each pair looked like Shiva and Parvati sitting together. Mahabhairavi with *chandas* was accompanying them. The *pretas* acted as bards and sang the *yogi*'s glory. While the procession was going on, the male fiends chattered, the ghosts laughed noisily, the *chandas* raised a war cry, the *yoginis* hooted, the betalas roared like lions and the followers of the *chandas* cheered. The sound of their cries was as deafening as the one coming out of the churning of the sea. It seemed as if they were breaking into the abode of *gandharvas* or like a heavy gust of wind sweeping away the clouds or another

Lakshmi emerging from a dirty sea. Anila Khechara, the commander of ghosts, Amukhya Kapalika, the commander of *preta*s, Jadumalla, the commander of wrestlers, Bhairimunda, the commander of *chanda*s, Kala Kalpa, the commander of *betala*s, Kapalapaisuna, the commander of the fiends, Dhumrasikha, the commander of warriors, Manibhadra, the commander of *yaksha*s, Raktaksha, the commander of *brahmadaitya*s, Kantimukha, the commander of the *guhyaka*s, Shivamukha, the commander of *yakshini*s and Mayasambhavi, the commander of the Matrukas took part in the procession. After seven days the journey ended when they reached the border of Prithi Tilak kingdom, one *kos* away from the exact destination.

There was a mango grove on the banks of the Uttam River where they stopped for rest. The *yogi* commanded Ratipriya *yakshini* to build a house there. Reciting Annapurna *mantra*, he arranged food for all: sacrificed animals for ghosts, water for *preta*s, heaps of flesh for *chanda*s, milk-cream for *betala*s, baked meat for *brahmadaitya*s, wine for wrestlers and vegetarian rice dishes for *yogi*s. Calling the *betala* Kankalamukha, he told him in confidence, 'Leave for the king's palace in disguise. Bring me a detailed information about the place where the woman is staying.' Carrying out his command, the *betala* disguised himself as a cat by using Ulluka Vidya and sneaked into the palace. Passing door after door, he reached where she was. As his eyes fell on her, he passed out. Regaining senses after a while, he mustered courage in him and said to himself, 'O she looks like Parvati! The earth must be proud of her. Why shouldn't the *yogi* have her?' He stayed there for four days. He ate things that cats are fond of. He kept vigil on the maiden closely and collected all information about her in the meantime.

On his return on the fifth day, the *betala* met Kamananda *yogi*. With folded hands, he said, 'Master! Carrying out your orders I entered the city secretly in disguise. That city was a sea of chariots, elephants, horses, soldiers and warriors. The air was filled with the sound of trumpets. The market places were spic and span. I saw beautiful women walking on the streets; their gait was like that of a swan. A large number of guards stood on watch at entry points. Chaturdrasta was keeping the Lion-Gates; at another gate a *yajna* was being performed. There were ten thousand white elephants, as big as mountains, there. The juice flowing from their temples had made the roads slippery. In addition, there were fast-moving horses deployed there. At some other entrance, there was the deployment of the royal staff. There were thousands of houses there, some shaped like umbrella, others beautifully designed, still others made of gold. The city was well protected. With great difficulty I managed to enter the inner circle of the palace where the young woman was staying. She was so beautiful that even Brahma, Indra and Rudra would not take their eyes off her. When I first saw her, I went into a swoon. My condition was like that of a pot of ghee melting in fire. I escaped from there unharmed somehow. That woman saw a handsome young man in her dream and fell in love with him. Chitrabati, her friend, who was also the minister's daughter, filled her in on every news of the young men of the city. She showed her many portraits to identify who, among them, was the man of her dream. But it was all in vain. At last she showed her the portrait of Rudra Sudhanidhi.

Seeing the portrait, she cast her head down with a blush. Filled with joy, she proclaimed him as the lord of her life. She hung it on the wall. The portrait looked like crystal; she adorned it with musk every day. She used to think of him day and night. She lost interest in everything else. She would press the portrait against her breasts; it made her feel like holding him in deep embrace. The maids would try to comfort her from time to time. The thought of Rudra Sudhanidhi occupied her mind entirely, which she could not overcome. This is all I had to tell you. Now decide what you should do.'

Hearing this, *yogi* Kamananda's passion for her became twice as much. It was as if a pot of ghee came in contact with fire. Overtaken by lustful desires, he called a meeting of the commanders to take their view on the subject. One of the commanders suggested to bring her forcibly. Another planned to buy her in exchange of wealth. Someone advised to exhibit jugglery. Someone suggested to cast a spell on her. There was another who proposed to possess the king and prevail on him to offer his daughter. Someone recommended to set the city on fire. Someone put forward the idea of possessing the boys of the city. Someone proposed to hypnotise her, and using *ulluka vidya*, carry her away with her bed. Someone suggested to take the help of magic. Someone proposed to create illusion. Someone recommended to possess her, drive away all others from the palace and carry her away. Someone suggested to kidnap her, making the whole city dark. Someone said boastfully that she must be fetched by any means and be the *yogi*'s wife. The *yakshini*s were of the view that they would prevail on her to come with them wilfully. Anila Khechara said, 'I will change myself to wind and sweep away the whole city. Kankalamukha, the *betala*, will be with me. While the city is in air, he will pick her'. The ghosts, who were listening to all this, said, 'Not to worry. We can carry away the city on our heads.' The chandas interrupted, 'We will fight and snatch her with an arrow'.

At last the *yogi* pronounced his verdict. He said, 'We will send a *brahmadaitya* to possess her and not leave her at all. I will visit her as an exorcist. I will prevail on her and bring her with me. The *brahmadaitya* will be with me. If he doesn't agree, I will take his life.' Saying so, he sent for the ghost army consisting of twelve thousand and eight hundred ghosts. He commanded them, 'Go and possess those in the inner palace. Some of you possess those in the palace, and others the subjects'. With a smile on his face, he ordered the *betala*s to unhitch the elephants and horses there. He instructed the chandas to raise a fire around the city. He asked the pretas to frighten the boys. He ordered the *yogini*s to raise a loud cry in the sky. He told Upasarpa, the *yakshini*, 'You will have to steal the elephants and horses and hold the soldiers captive'. He asked the *betalas* to make themselves invisible and roam about in the inner palace, threatening all those who come your way. He cautioned them not to take any food there. To Anila Khechara he said, 'Change yourself to a storm and sweep away the young woman like a piece of cotton'. He asked Ugrachandi to hide herself, and, in case there is any trouble, drop a hint at him. He ordered Brahmakumara Chanda to leave immediately and see that no hearth was lighted in any house. He asked Shakunu to throw all water-pots into water. To Suchimukha he assigned the job of making holes in each cooking pot and capture the woman at least opportunity. He told Saguni Chandi, 'Circle over the city with thousands of vultures. As a kite swoops on the flesh down under you pounce on her and lift the woman away when you see her.' He asked Bharija, a *yakshini*, to remove Lakshmi from the woman's shoulders. He advised Jadumalla to possess the king. He told the *pretas* to keep spreading fear until the woman was captured. He further ordered them to disturb everyone by sounding the horn made of cattle bone when they were asleep. He commanded Srugalamukha, a *chanda*, to disguise as a bear and prowl around the city, frightening the subjects. He instructed Istapada Matruka, 'Go to the river and turn to a beautiful boat studded with gems. Keep floating there. When she cames and sits on it, you would sink into water and fetch her to me.' To the sixty-four *yoginis* he said, 'You will serve as pavilions in the Totapura garden. When she sits on you fly her to me.' Assigning each their respective duties, the *yogi* sat back in brooding silence.

In obedience to the *yogi*'s command, all left for the city. Reaching there, they wreaked havoc there, the most affected being the inner palace. Outside, most houses stood empty as the inhabitants had fled the place in fear. The elephants were found straying in the city streets. The women had removed their clothes and tied them around their heads. The babies kept crying all the time. The royal flags were snapped. Many people were seen rolling over and over on the ground. Crows and jackals went on cawing and yelping day and night. Somewhere a regiment of soldiers stood helplessly; somewhere it was all dark. Some places were full of snakes, moving every which way. Men, women and children were crying in alarm. Women spilled on to the streets, anticipating that the city would be set to fire. Those courtiers, who were noble-minded, were pulled by the hair and tortured by the *betalas*. Some ghosts were lowing like the cattle and having sex with beautiful women, making them naked. The place resonated with a deafening noise, created by horses, elephants and the terrified subjects. Realizing the gravity of the situation, the subjects were fleeing the place in panic. Except a few who kept themselves indoors, other left for safe places. Some hid in trees, some inside water, some in the lofts of their houses and some in mountain caves. Some were cursing their fate while others were chanting 'Narasimha'. The *brahmadaitya*, in the meantime, was trying to influence the king, but was disappointed as the king was under Vishnu's protection. Yet he was not in a position to leave for fear of the *yogi*. Worried, the king prayed to Vishnu for help. He invoked the *sudarsan chakra* which was as radiant as crores of the sun, the source of all energy and most invincible. It was deployed there secretly by Vasudeva to provide protection for his followers. Suddenly it sprang to action, emitting just a spark, which was more than enough to finish off the enemy and save the kingdom from destruction.

Their bodies partly burnt, the ghosts scurried away, letting out a painful cry. Some of them passed out and lay where they were, as if dead. Regaining senses after a while, they flew away like birds in horror. The *brahmadaityas* were burnt to death in fire and the *yoginis* and *betalas* cried out 'Save us!' and fell unconscious for a moment. Soon after they hurried away in fear. The *pretas* were conveyed to heaven as they were killed in Vishnu's hands. Only those who survived, returned. They fell before the *yogi* with a thud. Someone was feeling a raging thirst. Someone was drinking water thirstily. Someone was wincing in pain. Someone was rubbing his half-burnt beard. Someone, leaving the *yogi*, was running to the forest. Someone was passing out again and again. Someone was in a state of dying. Someone was gritting his teeth. Someone was completely broken down in grief. Someone was asleep, his face down. Someone had singed his hair in the fire.

Seeing the army in disarray, the *yogi*'s face flushed with anger. He roved his eyes, looking like red water-lilies, over them. 'Who did all this to my army?' he roared out. He asked the *yogini*s about it. His beard half-burnt, the commander of ghosts replied with folded hands, 'O Lord! As instructed by you we went there and caused a lot of destruction in the city. Just when we were about to carry the woman away, an object looking like a wheel appeared in the sky. That was the wheel of death which created panic among our soldiers. Didn't I tell you before to go back and save our lives?' Hearing this, the *yogi* vowed, his head upraised, 'Wait! Wait! We will enquire about the wheel now. We must get the woman by hook or by crook since she is the cause of your misery.'

He sat in meditation invoking Chandi who appeared before him in no time. Her head was touching the sky. Her tongue was wagging; she was asking for food to eat. Her eyes looked like wheels of death; her tongue flashed like lightning and teeth as sharp as lances. Like a thunder clashing with another, she was rubbing her lips against each other, producing sparks. Her breath was so hot that the trees she passed by were burning, billowing smoke. A garland of human heads around her neck, she was dressed in red. Her body covered the whole sky and she was letting out a loud roar incessantly. Her feet did not touch the ground. Owls were emerging out of her teeth and she was roaring like a tiger, the sound of which was as deafening as the rumble of thunder. It seemed as if the roof of the universe was breaking into pieces. She had a scimitar in her hand. Groaning loudly, she appeared before the *yogi*. Seeing her, the *yogi* left his seat and lay prostrate before her. He begged her to devour the people of the city and fetch Abidya Mrutyusanjibani to him. With a loud roar like that of a thunderbolt, she rushed out. As she was about to enter the maiden's place, sparks of fire from the *sudarsan* showered on her and caught her hair and clothes which began to burn. She turned her head around and fell on the ground. It was like Indra clipping the mountain's wings. Suddenly the fire spread towards her. Scared, she plunged into the sea. There was no one to come to her rescue. Finally her body charred by half, she threw herself before the *yogi*, chanting 'O *dharma!*' Her miserable defeat made the *yogi* conclude that the last weapon he had had gone astray. He asked Anila Khechara what to do next. The ghost replied, 'You are our master; you are a devotee of Parvati who had wrapped the world in illusion. Her Lord, Shiva, overpowered by the *sudarsan*, had once surrendered to it. Can you sweep away the Meru by a blow of air from your mouth? Can a cat made of earth catch a snake? We can't do anything to neutralize the power of the wheel. Let's retreat and save our lives. Nevertheless I have a suggestion to make. That maiden is destined to marry Rudra Sudhanidhi who will bring her to this city. By that time the *sudarsan chakra* must have left the place. We will take advantage of it and abduct her in a moment's time.' The *yogi* consented; he decided to make friends with Rudra Sudhanidhi. He brought back the eyesight of his soldiers by reciting a *mantra*.

On his return to the Prithi Tilak kingdom, he took his seat on the Shakambari pavilion on the banks of the Amrit Tarangini River where his followers, filled with curiosity, gathered in large numbers. The city where Rudra Sudhanidhi lived was on the other side of the river. There was a ferry ghat nearby; the royal persons used to ferry across the river by boats. The boats were as huge as mountains and of various shapes and sizes. Some had brows like a crocodile's face, some had eight brows, some were triple decked, some were as big as the Himalayas, some were sail-boats and some were shaped like chariots. Some of those were decorated with flags. The boatmen were singing merrily. Some were eating baked cakes called *podapitha.* Some boats were bound for the city and sailed with oars. Kamananda Yogi approached the boatmen to ferry him across the river, but they refused to take him as he was a *tantrika.* In shame, Kamananda returned to his place and brought out a deer skin playfully. He spread it out on the river and got onto it. It moved faster than the boats, without sinking in water. All were amazed to see it.

How could he accomplish it? He tied a parasitic creeper to his ears. He allowed the inhaled air flow upwards and blocked its downward movement. He started *khechari-yoga* with *jalandhari* hand-posture, following rules of Kalpa Chintamani Vidya. He could produce many wonderful things out of nothing, which took the onlookers by surprise. What were the things he produced? They included metals, gems, fruits, medicine, clothes, jewellery, mirror, *pata* silk and food and cakes for children. He was also doing it on demand, that too, before everyone's eyes. His words were soft and polite that pleased everyone. He sat meditating on the sun. Invoking Bhairava, he ordered the deer skin to take him to the other bank. Reaching there in a moment, he jumped from his seat, withdrawing himself from the yogic exercises. The *betala*s hovered over him, making themselves invisible. He got onto the bank and sat on a pavilion there to which thousands of people flocked. They presented him with many kinds of offerings which the *yogi* gave away among the ghosts and *betala*s. Some of the people were happy to watch him, others learning *mantra*s from him, still others smearing their bodies with the holy ash given by him. He was regarded as a *siddha yogi* by one and all.

The *yogi* stayed there for a month, amazing the audience by his magical powers, but he was sorry to find that the news had not reached Rudra Sudhanidhi yet. In fact, none in the palace knew of it. So the *yogi* told Manoharini, one of the *yakshini*s, 'Go to Rudra Sudhanidhi immediately. Cast a spell on him and bring him here.' The *yakshini* left for the king's palace, and, after influencing the royal family, met Rudra Sudhanidhi. She informed him, 'A great *yogi* has come, the like of whom, was never seen before. He has been staying in our city. He has travelled many cities and kingdoms. A handsome-looking young man with shoulder-length hair, he is an authority on many subjects.' Impressed by her words, he called Gunashila, son of Bibeka Ratnakar, the minister, and told him, 'Dear friend! I wish to see the *yogi*.' Gunashila was as wise as Brihaspati. His face was like that of the moon, conscience like that of Varuna, voice like that of Sarasvati, speed like that of the wind, knowledge like that of Vighnesvar, radiance like that of fire, learning like that of Vyasa and knowledge of sculpture like that of Vishvakarma. He was an epitome of virtues by the blessings of Vasudeva. He protested, 'O Lord! You are as great as Indra. It is not desirable to visit a *tantrika*. Long ago Gorekhnath and many other *siddha yogi*s had attained their salvation through meditation and prayers. They left behind the *tantrika shastra*s to befool the wicked ones. No matter how dedicated the *tantrika*s might be, they would never give up their bodily desires. They derive pleasure out of it. They choose this as they fear to undergo the hardship required for salvation. Such false practices encourage sinful actions. Our scriptures prohibit us from visiting a *tantrika* whimsically.' Hearing this, the prince replied, 'What's wrong in it? *Siddha*s appear in many forms. Inscrutable are the ways of God. In Sri Purusottama Kshetra, *siddha*s have their families; they involve themselves in worldly affairs, still they take *nirmalya*. Some of them attain salvation, others are conveyed to the abode of Vishnu. Dear friend! God's *maya* is beyond human comprehension. This is what the *Vishnu Purana* says. Don't have second thoughts. Get the troops and chariots ready. We will go in chariots. Hurry up! We should not keep him waiting. It is a virtue to see the unseen.' The minister's son consented to it.

By that time it was evening already. The flood of moonlight made the earth look like crystal. No sooner was it light than the prince and his friend ascended the chariot. How did the chariot look? Decked in many kinds of flowers, it had a roof studded with gems of the kinds that used to melt in moonlight into dews. The morning warmed into a hot day. It seemed like lotuses sprinkling honey all over. As the chariot took off, it looked like the second day moon of autumn. Below it, a complete army was marching, surrounding the chariot that looked like a mountain peak in spring. Leading from the front was a regiment of foot-soldiers who were looking like an ambush of tigers. All of them were young, handsome and capable. They fought like cocks, raising their legs into the air. They were as ferocious as lions. They were looking like huge mountain peaks. They were twenty-five years in age, each armed with a pair of iron chains. They could run five *yojana*s at a stretch just for fun. Each of them used to drink the milk of ten buffaloes every day. If they pulled on the bow-string, the bow would break into pieces. They could shoot at a mustard seed successfully. They could pull a trumpet of elephants by the legs. Even a horse worth one lakh rupees would not compete with them in running. They would jump into the battlefield like insects to fire. Behind them were the elephants looking like rain clouds. Extremely fearful, those elephants had eyes like the rising sun; they went wild round the year. They could withstand thunder. They had twenty toes each and right-facing teeth. They were like Yama to the foes. Their tails were white. They were as mighty as they were fearless. They could dig a mountain with their tusks. They had large bodies, thick shoulders shaped like urns. Once provoked, they would rush into fire. In rut, the juice from their crowns would flow profusely. The silver chains on them looked like snakes intertwined. With *chamaras* on them, they looked like yaks showing their white tails or like burying themselves in garlands of tinkling bells. They were of metal complexion. When their bells tinkled it sounded like gusts of wind rushing into a cave. They presented the picture of a beautiful sea.

Dressed gorgeously, the mahouts were sitting on the back of the elephants hitting their goads at their ears and tapping on the sides of their crowns. They were moving in style. Behind them were the fast-moving horses of the best breed who would beat the wind by speed. While racing they looked like the sly glances of a clever woman. While galloping some were taking a curved line, some gazing at the sky, some running faster than others and some flashing like lightning. They appeared as beautiful as a constellation of stars. The mahouts were kicking them with their legs from time to time. Such was the procession of Rudra Sudhanidhi. Dolled up in *pata* silk, he had the bow and arrow in his hands, a roll of chrysanthemum flowers around his bun, marks of musk on his forehead, a pearl necklace hanging from his neck, a belt of gems around his neck and a waist-belt studded with four kinds of gems. As he moved, flowers were strewn on him, incense burnt, and bugles were blown. It seemed as if Kamadeva had descended on the earth. After travelling long, the journey stopped at the Vinayak Mandapa on the border of the city. It was in the holy land of Kanchanasthali. The *mandapa* was made of *darpana* stones. It was two kos wide and located on the banks of the Amrit Tarangini River. It looked like a garland around the earth's neck. There were green shoots of plants around it that looked like human beings. Hearing the news of the arrival of the army, the commander of ghosts informed the *yogi*, 'O Lord! Sarbamanoharini *yakshini* whom you had sent to the king's place has brought Rudra Sudhanidhi here by fraud and guile.'

Filled with joy, the *yogi* started the practice of Mohana Vidya. Fixing his eyes on the tip of his nose, straightening his spine, contracting the navel and sitting in a lotus pose, he looked like an enlightened *yogi*. Knowing that Rudra Sudhanidhi was arriving very shortly, he invoked Upasarpa *yakshini*, and using Jalandhar *tantra*, had an army, as large as that of the prince, made by her. Surrounded by *yoginis* and soldiers, he was looking like a cloud of smoke in the abode of the *gandharvas*; the whole sight seemed to be an addition to the beauty of Kanchanasthali and the river. Seeing the troops, someone of the prince's party exclaimed, 'What! There was no one here till now. Where did all these come from? Is it an invasion force intending to usurp our land?' At this, the warriors picked their bow and arrow and got ready to face the challenge. Amazed to see all this, the prince and the minister's son placed before the *yogi* the offerings they had brought with them and lay prostrate before him. The *yogi* raised them to their feet and asked them to take their seats. He, then, applied Kalandi *tantra* which consigned Gunashila's wit and wisdom into oblivion. The *yogi* was quite confident of his spiritual power. Stunned by the handsome appearance of the prince, he mused, 'The earth has nothing fairer than this!' The sixty-four *yoginis*, *yakshinis* and Matrukas were also bewitched by it. Anila Khechara whispered, 'This youngman has enchanted the three worlds. It is for him that Parvati produced the maiden from her body. Keep him amused. Once he reposes faith in you, take the woman away. There is no fear of the *sudarsan* wheel in this city.'

To impress Rudra Sudhanidhi, the *yogi* sat down, his eyes shut. The prince asked, 'Where did you come from?' The *yogi* replied, 'My son! We were in Puspagiri. After taking a holy dip in Triveni, we ended our fast.' The prince asked, 'What is your age?' 'Equal to the number of stars in the sky', was the answer. The minister's son enquired, 'Where were you staying previously?' The *yogi* said, 'It is where you see me. Isn't it absurd to ask this to someone who has created the world?' The prince whispered to his friend, 'He must be a *yogi* of the highest order. Today is the luckiest day for us, on which we extolled the virtues of meeting such a great soul.' The *yogi* suggested, 'Let me show something to both of you'. Asking all others to stay where they were, the threesome walked on until they saw a strange palace before them. Its gates, made of sapphire, were bigger than the height of two elephants, one upon the other. On both sides of it, there stood two blocks of houses made of crystal and attended by one thousand maids. Seeing the *yogi*, the maids bowed to him respectfully and made way for him. The prince and his friend were taken aback to see all this. They wondered, 'Never had we seen such a place existing here before! It was not there yesterday when we passed this way on hunting. Where did this wonderful structure fall from?' They could not ask the *yogi* about it lest it might hamper their close friendship. Studded with gems, the doors looked like naked women. One of the maids took the prince inside and showed him everything—a huge number of women and plenty of wealth. She led him the way to a pond, in the middle of which, there was a platform. She sat the prince on it and ordered her companions to bathe both of the friends. At this, a gaggle of glamorous women dressed them up gorgeously. After massage and bath, they combed and braided their hair. They decked them in jewellery and *pata* silk. They took them to the inner palace passing a number of doors.

At one door they saw a gathering of heavenly conveyances, at another a trumpet of wild elephants on guard. Some doors were guarded either by chariots or horses of the best breed or courtiers or distinguished warriors. There was a door where the maids were busy serving the *yogi* and at another, a music session was being held. As the *yogi* passed door after door, the maids bowed to him and strewed flowers on him. There were many kinds of performances going on there, such as wrestling, paruahata, sheep fighting, religious debates and devotional music. Next they came across a house which looked like Alakapura. Maids, with lamps in their hands, were standing there. In moonlight, their clothes looked as if wet.

As they reached there the cooks served them eighty-four dishes. After meals the maids fanned them and entertained them with a dance performance. The *yogi* was sitting on a bed while the two friends were on another. They were not sure whether what they saw was illusion or truth. They thought the *yogis* must be superior to the kings. In respect of wealth, the kings were much poorer than the *yogis*. While they were brooding over such thoughts, the *yogi* said, 'My sons! This is my hermitage. Do come sometimes. You will like it, all your sins will be redeemed. Now you may return to your place. Take cold food and retire to bed. If your devotion to me is true, you will find me here when you wish.' Saying so, he offered them cloth and jewellery and bade them farewell. The two friends expressed their gratitude to him and returned to the city with their army.

On reaching home, Rudra Sudhanidhi bowed to the king and told him all about the *yogi* and the miracles he created. The king told him, 'Meet him tomorrow morning and fetch him here. We will request him to stay with us for some days. We will entertain him with great hospitality. Let's first examine whether his acts are illusion or not. If we find his acts fraudulent, we will finish him off.' Next morning the prince, riding a horse, reached the *yogi*'s place. It was early morning. There was no trace of the palace there. He found the *yogi* lying on a heap of ash. A stream of semen was flowing out as a mark of his last night's sexual intercourse. He was in the guise of a monkey and looking around with flipping eyes. As the prince went near him he awoke and sat straight. He smeared his body with ash, and, using Mohana Vidya, hypnotized the prince. With folded hands, the prince said, 'O sage! I see no one here!' The *yogi* explained, 'Everyone is here, but they are invisible. You can't see them even if I show them to you. It is something divine.' The prince begged him, 'I wish to ask for a boon. Kindly grant it.' To which the *yogi* replied, 'Tell me what you wish to have. We are one. I inhabit every soul. Why would you pray to me if I don't oblige you?' The prince said benignly, 'I implore you to come to our house and stay with us for four days.' The *yogi* responded, 'To us, staying in the palace is as good as living in a cremation ground. We don't differentiate between a forest and a house. Places don't matter. In return for your devotion to me, I will keep your request and stay at your place for a few days. You go ahead of me.'

He, then, called the *betalas* and commanded them to take him to the palace. 'Let four of you attend my four sides. Go slowly, so that no one will recognize you.' With those instructions, he sat in lotus posture. When the *betalas* carried him through the air, people thought that some *siddha yogi* was travelling in the sky. His followers were moving behind him in circles. The prince followed them, riding a horse. Flowers were being strewn on the *yogi* off and on. He was speaking softly and looking around with roving eyes. Down under, children were running among the crowd with the hope of getting cakes as they used to have on earlier occasions. The doe-eyed women were peeping through the windows to have a glimpse of it. It seemed to them as if a *yogi* was being worshipped in a sea of blue water-lilies. The spectacular sight of the *yogi*'s journey seemed to enchant the three worlds. The commander of ghosts was holding a royal umbrella that looked like floating in the air. This way, Kamananda Yogi reached the lion-gates of the palace. When, after passing five doors, he reached the king, he was surprised to see his throne. Greatly amazed to see the *yogi* coming in the air, the king left his seat and rushed forward to receive him. He offered him a seat and worshipped him with welcome rituals. 'He must be a *siddha yogi*', he thought, 'Or else, how could he journey through the air? I have never seen such a yogi before.' Again he thought, 'What has a *siddha yogi* got do with men? It seems mysterious. Well! We will know all about him when we communicate with him.'

The king's silence aroused suspicion in the *yogi*'s mind. He ordered Yakshini Karnapisachi to tell him what the king was thinking about. The *yakshini* read his mind quickly and whispered to the *yogi* what the king was feeling about him. The *yogi* turned to the king and said, 'O King of kings! In my view you are wrong. You question why a *yogi* should visit men. Don't you know that great sages such as Lomasha, Parashara, Vasistha and Vishvamitra visited kings very often? *Siddhas* like Gorakh and Matsyendra had saved many kings from ruination'. Stunned by the *yogi*'s power to read his mind, he worshipped him out of fear. He put a garland around his neck, smeared his body with *aguru*, *kumkum*, camphor and musk and gazed at him wonderingly. Just then, the *yogi* smeared his forehead with some *ulluka bibhuti* that made him invisible. The prince and others were worried; they thought that the *yogi* disappeared because of the king's suspicion on him. They felt sorry for having gambled away a rare opportunity. Finding them repentant of what they had done, the *yogi* wiped his forehead and reappeared on the gem-studded bed. The king worshipped at his feet and others followed suit. They acknowledged him as God. They offered him many valuable gifts to pacify his anger. It was then that Madhu and Malati, two singers, entered there. The pair looked like the Moon-God and Rohini or like Kamadeva and Rati.

They had long arms and wide chests. They were adorned with garlands and many kinds of ornaments. What did Madhu look like? Dressed in green, he had tucked many kinds of flowers to his bun. He was chewing betel with comphor and standing in a triple-bend pose, with the *veena* in his hands. How was Malati? She had put on a fine cloth with folds and had her bun tilted to the left. The cloth that covered her breasts was held together by clips. As she bent her body in different poses, beads of sweat appeared on her. With a faint smile on her lips and her sly glances, she enchanted everyone. She was as beautiful as the tail of a *kajalapati* bird and was washing her face with scented water. It seemed as if the full moon had descended on the earth. The words she spoke smilingly seemed like a cascade of nectar tumbling down from her lips. Seeing them dressed like *gandharva* and apsara, the king told himself, 'How shall I describe this man? We may say he is a *vidyadhara*, but his feet are touching the ground. The flowers in his garland are fading. The coat of sandalwood paste on his body is drying up. So, by no means he is from heaven. We may say he hails from Nagaloka, the land of snakes, but he has neither a hood nor a jewel on it. Therefore we conclude that he is a man of the earth'. With this in mind, he asked Madhu, 'Hey man! Whose glory do you sing? What is so special about you? Who do you serve? If you know something extraordinary, speak it out.'

The singer replied, 'O King of kings! The one I am singing about can catch the three worlds in the snare of her beauty. If all are *chakora*, she will be the moon. She is the flag flying on the chariot of Kamadeva, the conqueror of the fourteen worlds. She is the lightning among the clouds of women. She is like a lamp for those who grope in the darkness for love. She is the boat in the sea of Ananga. Rarest of the rare, she is the source of joy, passion of love and wealth. She is the daughter of a king who is the devotee of a great sage. Words fail to describe her beauty.' Saying so, the singer called Madhu invoked Sri Ganesha and Sarasvati, cleared his throat, took medicine such as *brahmamandi*, *bacha*, *sunthi*, *sarkara*, *pippali*, honey and *nilakanthamula* and began singing with Malati in Malava Raga. The song was the glorification of the maiden's beauty and virtues:

'That jewel of a woman is a king's daughter. She has a slender waist; her face is like the moon, voice like that of a cuckoo, eyes like that of a doe, gait like that of a wild elephant and words like nectar. An enchantress of the three worlds, she has all the attributes of Manmath. She is as fragrant as a lotus in bloom. Clad in yellow and ochre clothes she has a gold complexion that make her look like the lightning. Her face bears a smile that would bewitch Kandarpa. She can disturb the mind of a *yogi* in meditation. She is another Lakshmi, a symbol of prosperity and immortality. Shesanaga could describe her beauty only if she were awake day and night, like the snake. The Moon-God could have done it had he not the periods of wax and wan. Kamadeva could have narrated it if he were not overpowered by her beauty. The Wind-God could have done it were her breasts not swinging under her clothes. Sarasvati might be able to do it had she not been busy playing the *veena* before Narayan. Brihaspati could have narrated it if the Venus were in the right position in her horoscope. Sanatkumar could have done it if he weren't underage. Basuki could have been of great help if she weren't carrying the earth on her head. Himalaya would have said it if he weren't very cold. The Milky Sea might have been able to do it if it weren't churned.

Failing to describe the maiden's beauty, all the gods flocked to Brahma for his advice. They asked him about how to assess the beauty and virtues of Abidya Mrutyusanjibani Karani. Brahma said, 'Well! The Milky Sea can't be her equal in beauty as it produces many undesirable things. How can the Moon-God be her match when he himself is not spotless and loses his lustre during the daytime? A lotus can't be a parallel to her as it decays when the dew falls on it. Kandarpa's mirror, no matter how clear it is, can't be taken into consideration as it is made of metal, which is hard and dull. We may consider the case of the Amrit Sarovara, but it has no running water. She can't be said to be Madana's abode as Madana hides in her navel in fear of her sidelong glances. The question of comparing her to Rati does not arise as the latter looks like her maid in her presence. She is also not like a snare which fails to catch her breasts in it. Like those of Kamadeva, her cheeks are shaped like the crescent moon, eyes like a pair of lotus flowers and pupils like bumble bees. Her eyebrows are like the *kodanda*, nose like a til flower and lips like *badhuli* flowers, shining red and looking like burning fire. Her lips seem to be overflowed by streams of nectar. In spite of many similarities, she can't be compared with conch because the conch, collected from the Milky Sea, is hard and unfeeling in nature. The *parijata* flower smells sweet only when it blooms, but, like the *champaka*, she is fragrant all the time. We can't say her teeth resemble the *kaustubha* gem as the gem has a hole in it. Her gait is not the same as that of the Narmada which is slow-moving. Nor can we compare it with that of an elephant because the elephant is scared of demons and firearms. Her earlobes look like the wheel that Hari carries in his hand. Her breasts can't be said to be the same as the round protuberances on the elephant's brow because the latter is hairy. The sight of her sweet lips fill the onlookers with immense joy. The Milky Sea will fall short of the virtues she possesses.' Unable to find a definite conclusion, the creator was at his wit's end. Therefore, he sat in meditation until he alighted on a series of brilliant simile to describe her beauty:

'Unlike the steady flow of the Kalandi River, her hair is like the reflection of the new monsoon clouds on the waves of the sea of nectar. It is more beautiful than the musk-smeared breasts of the *apsaras*. It can't be compared with gold which does not move. It is like the shadow of peacock's plume on the seashore. It does not look like the emerald either. It has the mixed colour of blue water-lily and blue lotus. Had the Yamuna been wavy it would have some likeness with her hair. Doesn't it look like the *chamara* in Kandarpa's Tailokya Bijaya chariot? Her upper lip looks like Kandarpa's bow or like a garland in the shape of the half moon or like her arched eyebrow. Its design is so marvellous that it will put Vishvakarma, Demon Maya and Brihaspati to shame. Look at her mouth. We can't compare it with Amrit Shila as it has no passion for love. Nor can we say it is a touchstone simply because it does not sweat with feelings of love. We, too, won't say it is free spirit because it does not move from one place to another. It can't be considered a letter written by Kandarpa with *kumkum* as it has no letters. We can't call it the rising moon because the moon does not appear by the day. Lord Shiva carries half the moon on his forehead; the other half he made into a golden boat, inverted it and formed her forehead with it. There is a dot of vermilion on it. How does it look? Does it look like

Mohini Lakshmi's smile? Or like the moon rising in the sky of love? Or has Manmath, dispelling the darkness, created a red lotus in the sea of nectar? Or Kandrapa, after being burnt in fire by Lord Shiva, was rising again to life? Below that dot of vermilion were wisps of hair looking like a net spread out by Manmath. Flopping in the wind, it looks like the flags of a king. Is it to enchant the youth of the three worlds? Is it the autumn moon emerging out of the sable clouds? Or like the flashes of lightning in the golden hued clouds?

Her eyebrows are curved, thick, well-shaped and beautiful. They look as charming as Kandarpa's floral *chamaras* or as a pair of black snakes or as emerald creepers or as a necklace made of sapphire. They look like the stain on the moon. They are the lines drawn to solve the dispute between Rahu and the bumble bees. Do they represent the sixty-four ways of making love? Or are they letters written by Kamadeva in musk on the face of the moon?

Words fail to describe the beauty of her eyes. A mere thought of it will make a man mute. Decorated with collyrium, they are as roving as those of the *khanjana* bird. Their beauty will put the blue water-lilies, the doe and the waves to shame. They ridicule even the beauty of the lotus. They are not like the waters of the blue ocean because of its warmth. It is not like the blue water-lily which fades, nor like the young doe which is unaware of the feelings of love, nor like the ocean of lust that is not everlasting. They can't be compared with the waves of the Kalandi as they have a slow movement, nor with the waves of the sea in the full moon night because of its loud roar. It is not the same as an arrow of passion which leaves the bow when fired. We can't compare her eyes with a pair of *safari* fish as they don't smell sweet. They are not like the *khanjana* bird which is extremely agile. We can't call them bubbles of nectar which stay only for a moment. Neither collyrium nor sapphire qualifies to be their equal. They can't be said to be oysters as they are not steady. They can't be a pair of *chakora* who suffers from the pangs of separation.

The lotuses don't deserve a comparison as her eyes are not weeds that grow on water. They are not like the waves of the Ganga which is dirty, nor like Kandarpa's mirror which is not so clean. We can't describe them as nectar as the latter is not visible. They are not parallels to parrots who always go on talking. It is absurd to compare her to a lamp as the lamp has oil in it. They are fairer than the dew, icy waters of the Ganga, *kunda* flowers, water-lily, lotus, milk, conch , pearl and snow-all white things taken together. They are more attractive than those of Kamadeva. The Creator had prepared a mixture in a pot of nectar, adding all things that were blue-black in colour, in a dark night. Those things were musk, gold, the blue from *nilakantha* bird's neck, emerald, rain-cloud, colour of the peacock, bumble bee, the stain of the moon and waters of the Yamuna. After heating all those, he prepared a mixture and painted two blue water-lilies with it, decorating its sides with Kandarpa's flower-arrows. That is how he made her eyes which enchanted Kamadeva.

What to speak of her nose? It is sharp, straight and beautiful to look at. Both of the nostrils are elevated and symmetrical which breathe air in and out. Her nose swells as she breathes; it looks as if a *ketaki* flower is in bloom with the touch of wind. It looks as if made of gold that is melted five times. Seems as if Madana has raised his sword to sever the minds of the youth. Or is it a til flower made of gem hanging with its head bent low? Or is it a handle to whisk the nectar in the churner made by Maya, the demon? Or is it a *parijata* bud created by Vishvakarma? Or a beautiful passage made by Kandarpa, that exudes the honey of love? Or is it a house where Kamadeva hides in fear of her sly glances? It is as delicate as a *sirisa* flower. It seems like Lord Venus sucking nectar from the disc of the full moon. It looks like a fruit growing on the creeper of love and its juice dripping on the swing on the full moon day. It looks like the royal fan of Kandarpa. Seeing it, Kamadeva has turned his face away from Rati. Seems as if it is meant for making the youth suffer.

How do her lips look like? They look like a crimson-coloured leaf full of juice. It is as if a river full of the foam of nectar or the outline of a lotus flower or the flower of the *badhuli* plant grown by Lakshmi. What should we call it? Can it be a buoy of pomegranate flowers to ferry across the sea of sorrow? Or something that captivates the mind and eyes and creates the passion of love? Or a half-visible rising sun? Or a garland of red flowers hanging over the chest of the king of seasons? Or a boat made of gems entering the sea of lust on the waters of her sly glances? Or a flash of lightning in the clouds of golden colour? Or *badhuli* flowers enchanting the mind? Or a river of gems that charms the hearts of the youth? We can't compare it with *bimba* fruit as the latter has a tinge of ochre; nor with the *badhuli* flower which takes a long time to bloom, nor with *palasha* flower which blooms part by part. It can't be the pomegranate flower as its colour doesn't exactly match with it. It is not the same as coral because it is not hard. It can't be said to be like the parrot's beak which is a bit pale in colour, nor like the rising sun because of its warmth. It is not like a gem as it blooms slowly. It can neither be compared with the lotus which has pollen grains, nor with a roaring fire which is doused by water. It can't be said to be cut by scissors which is used to lace the beads into a garland. It can't be equal to the evening cloud which is swift in movement, nor to the red lotus as it blooms on the surface of water. It can't be parallel to the first day moon which is very cold. It is neither the same as *parijata* nor red water-lily. We can't compare it with vermilion which doesn't sweat. To make it Vishvakarma collected the colour of water-lily, pomegranate flower and *parijata*, the softness of fruits, the shine of coral, the redness of the parrot's beak and that of fire. He mixed these up in presence of Lakshmi and added juice of leaves of *kalpalata* creeper, the colour of gems and the mirth of spring to it. With all these ingredients, Vishvakarma made her lips. Its redness surpassed that of the blood.

How is her voice? It is as sweet, passionate, soft and soothing as the sound of Manmath's flute. Is it a *mantra* to destroy Kandarpa's boastfulness? Is it meant for the great *yogis* to develop their concentration of mind? Is it like the sound of the river of love falling into the sea of joy? Is it the sound of the *veena* coming from Kandarpa's flower-bow? Or the gurgling sound of the sea of beauty? Or the cause of Madana's new creations? Or the dispeller of the darkness of lust? Or a means to make the light of the lamp brighter? Is it to soak the trees burnt by the fire of lust with nectar? Or to instil a tune in the flute of love? Or the sound of Manmath's conch announcing his victory over the three worlds? Or the chuckling sound of the tongue during sexual intercourse? Or the buzzing sound of the bumble bee of Madana's mind around a face looking like lotus? How should we define the quality of her voice? It can't be compared with the sound of Kandarpa's conch because it is much louder. Her voice is not like that of Manmath's flute as it has nine holes, nor of the parrot, bumble bee and cricket. It is not equal to that of the cuckoo which sings only in spring, so also to the sound of the flute which is not solemn.

Considering all this, the creator took the soft musical note from Sarasvati's veena, the buzz of the bees, the chirp of crickets, the first tune of the flute, the grave tune of conch, the sweet note of the parrot, the musical note of the drum, the sound of the autumn clouds and the lighter note of Manmath's harp and mixed all those in nectar in equal proportions. Reciting Mrutyusanjibani mantra, he added to the mixture the voice of the male cuckoo and all grammatical rules of music resulting in the creation of a new voice that is cool, calm, soothing and melodious. That is the voice she possesses. It seems as if the moon has risen to remove the darkness of lustful desire. Or like the Milky Sea simmering in light. Or like the flame of love burning the hearts of young men. Seeing her beauty, Kamadeva shot his arrow at the gods, instead. It took every life into its thrall. Manmath filled the mountain of clouds with beauty.

How are her rows of teeth? We may say it is the crystal rosary of Kandarpa, but it doesn't hold good as the beads of the rosary are meant to roll. We may call it the seeds of pomegranate, but it is not as soft and as moist. We may compare it to diamond, but it is not as shining as her teeth. It is not like gem which is devoid of the passion of love. We may say it is like the brushing of evening clouds against the rising moon. . . .

Glossary

aguru	:	a scented paste of a kind of sandalwood used as cosmetic
abadhuta	:	a Shaivite mendicant
Achyuta	:	imperishable, Krishna
Ambika	:	Parvati
anahata	:	The fourth of the six *chakras* that exists in the heart, represented by a lotus with twelve petals
apsara	:	a celestial damsel
Astavakra	:	Son of sage Kohada and Sujata, the daughter of Sage Uddalaka. While in the womb he pointed out the mistakes of his father in the recitation of Vedic *shlokas*, for which his father cursed him. Eight (*asta*) curves appeared in his body as a result of the curse. He authored *Astabakra Samhita*, a *shastra* based on *yoga*
atman	:	self; individual soul
betala	:	a follower of Lord Shiva
Bhargava	:	a descendant of sage Bhrigu
Bhubanesvari	:	one of the ten *tantrika* incarnations of Goddess Durga
bibhuti	:	holy ash; a symbol of divinity
bimba	:	a creeper; its fruit looks shining red when it is ripe
Bishrava	:	a sage; Ravana's father
Bishvakarma	:	also Vishvakarma; the chief architect of heaven

Brahman	:	the Ultimate Reality underlying all phenomena
bramharandhra	:	the imaginary hole on the top of the skull through which the life-force of *yogi*s leaves the body
Brihaspati	:	Jupiter; the teacher of the gods in Hindu mythology
chakra	:	centre of energy in the subtle body along the spinal axis through which consciousness manifests in human form. These are *muladhara*, *svadhisthana*, *manipura*, anahata, bisuddhi and ajna.
chakravaka	:	also *chakora*; a bird said to be living on moonlight
chakravarti	:	emperor
chamara	:	chowrie; a long brush made of tufts of the tail-hair of a yak, used as a fan or a fly-whisk
chandrayana	:	a religious vow and penance consisting of regulating one's daily diet by gradual diminution for the first fifteen days of the lunar month and gradual increment for the next lunar fortnight and observing continence and self-control
Charvaka	:	a sage; the propounder of the materialistic or aesthetic system of Hindu philosophy
chatasali	:	a village school run by *abadhan*s (teacher) in pre-modern Odisha
Chhaya	:	one of the two wives of Sun-God; the other one was Samjna
chid	:	pure intelligence
chintamani	:	the philosopher's stone
Dakini, Hakini, Bakini, Kakini	:	followers of Goddess Kali
Daksha	:	one of Brahma's sons and the progenitor of mankind

damaru : *dambaru* in Odia; a small double-faced drum in the shape of an hour-glass, associated with Lord Shiva; here cosmic heartbeat

Damodara : Vishnu

Devaki's Son : Krishna

dharma : an act of conduct approved by scriptures

dikpala : the gods ruling the ten directions. According to Manu they are Kubera, Indra, Bayu, Yama, Varuna, Agni, the Moon, the Sun, Brahma and Vishnu. The Vedas mention five *dikpala*s and the Buddhists four

dundubhi : a drum

Eight supreme divine powers : (Sanskrit: *asteischarya*); *anima*, *laghima*, *mahima*, *vyapti*, *prakamya*, *isita*, *bisita* and *kama*

Ekamra grove : Bhubaneswar, Odisha

fifty alphabets : Odia language has forty-nine alphabets. Here one more addition to it which is *om*

five vital airs : *prana*, *apana*, *byana*, *udana* and *samana*

forty-nine airs : forty-nine forms of air born to Aditi; violent pantings before death.

fourteen worlds : the universe imagined as composed of fourteen layers, seven below the earth (*atala*, *vitala*, *sutala*, *rasatala*, *talatala*, *mahatala* and *patala*) and seven above it (*bhuh*, *bhuvah*, *swah*, *mahah*, *janah*, *tapah* and *satya*)

Ganapati : Lord Ganesha

ganas : the retinue of Lord Shiva

gandharvas : demi-gods

Garuda : a huge mythological bird born to sage Kashyapa and Binita. He was a great Vaishnava and the carrier of Vishnu. The king of birds, he had large wings and a big nose

Gayatri : the most powerful of all *mantras*; the mother of the four Vedas

Girija : Parvati; so called as she was the daughter of Mountain (*giri*), the Himalayas

Gorakh : Gorakhnath; a Natha *yogi* and a powerful exponent of *yoga marga*

graha : (Indian mythology) planet

hatha-yoga : a *tantrika* from of Yoga

Hidimba : sister of demon Hidimba (*ka*); Bhimasen killed Hidimba and married her

humours : the liquids that were thought in the past to be in a person's body and to influence health and character

ida : also *inla*; an energy channel that starts from the left testicle and ends in the left nostril. It symbolizes feminine energy and causes a cooling effect in the body.

jambura : an instrument for catching a thing strongly

jatharagni : the digestive fire in the belly, causing gastric heat

Jyotisashastra : a book dealing with astrology

kaivalya : the state of absolute freedom

kalpabata : the legendary banyan tree which survives a Kalpa

kalpamahausadhi : a yogic way to free one's mind from all desires

Kamadeva : God of love. He was Brahma's son who was burnt alive by Lord Shiva for disturbing in his meditation. Later he was gramted life, but not the body, for which he was called. Atanu or Anarga. Some of his other names are Mara, Kandarpa, Manasija, Madana, Manmath, Pradyumna, Makaradhvaja, Minaketana and Darpaka. He carries a bow and five arrows and strikes them at young

		men, women and animals to arouse their sexual desire.
Kamadhenu	:	a fabulous cow that grants its possesser everything he wishes.
Kandarpa's mirror	:	Kandarpa had a mirror through which every object looked beautiful
Kailas	:	a mountain in Odisha where Lord Shiva is worshipped; here a substitute for the Kailas
karma	:	the law of cause and effect
Karttikeya	:	also Karttik, Kumar and Skanda; Lord Shiva's son
Ketu	:	the ninth planet of Hindu astrology; an evil omen
khatvanga	:	a long, studded club used as a weapon
kinnara	:	singers of heaven with bodies of men and heads of horses
kodanda	:	Ram's bow
kos	:	two miles approximately
konta	:	a weapon with a sharp head
kshatriya	:	one of the major castes in Hindu society, the other three being brahmin, vaishya and shudra
Kubera	:	Bishrava's son; the custodian of wealth in heaven
kumbhaka	:	retention of breath in *pranayama*
kumkum	:	a red cosmetic
kundalini	:	potential energy lying dormant in *muladhara*; coiled up energy
landabaguli	:	an unattractive white-coloured flower
lila	:	God's cosmic playfulness
linga	:	(Hinduism) a symbol of divine generative energy, especially a phallus and phallic object as symbol of Shiva
Lomasha	:	a sage; younger brother of sage Markandeya

mandapa	:	a platform which is open on all sides, usually attached to a temple
Manu	:	a sage; author of *Manu Samhita*
Matsyendranath	:	also macchendranath, Minapa; originator of Natha Shaiva lineages; adiguru of the Nath cult
maya	:	illusion
Maya demon	:	Ravana's father-in-law and Mandodari's father
merudanda	:	the spinal cord
Meru mountain	:	the Meru mountain of mythological fame. It is also called Hemadri, Sumeru, Ratnasanu and Amaradri. It is 84 thousand *yojana*s in height of which 16 thousand *yojana*s are submerged. It has three mounts. It finds a mention in *Bhagavata, Nrusimha Purana* and *Kurma Purana.* In modern geography, it is the North Pole located in the Arctic circle.
Mimansa	:	a philosophical system invented by Jaimini
Mohini Kanya	:	an enchantress
mudra	:	specific hand-postures created to facilitate the flow of energy, *prana* in the body and mind for optimal health.
nadi	:	energy channels through which *prana* air moves. There are a total of seventy-two thousand *nadi*s in human body of which the three most important ones are *inla* (*ida*), *pingala* and *sushumna.*
Nagas	:	name of a dynasty
Nanda's son	:	Krishna
Nilachala	:	Puri, the abode of Lord Jagannatha
nirmalya	:	the dry form of boiled rice offered to Lord Jagannatha

nine kinds of bhakti	:	*Shravana*, *kirtana*, *smarana*, *padasevana*, *archana*, *bandana*, *paricharya*, *sakhya* and *dasya*
nirvana	:	salvation; liberation; beatitude
Padmini	:	*Kamashastra* divides women into four groups, the best of them is Padmini.
panchajanya	:	Srikrishna's conch
Panchanana	:	one with five heads; Lord Shiva
Pandu's sons	:	the Pandavas
paramahamsa	:	a title conferred on an ascetic of highest order
Pasupata	:	a branch of Hindu philosophy propounded by the Shaivite *yogi*s
Patanjali	:	a great sage; the author of a *shastra* on *yoga* which is divided into four parts: *yogapada*, *sadhanapada*, *bibhutipada* and *kaivalyapada*
Pinaka	:	also Ajanga and Ajagaba; Shiva's bow
pingala	:	a *nadi* on the right side of the spine
prakriti	:	primordial Nature; the ultimate cause of the material world; comprised of *sattva*, *rajas* and *tamas*, the three qualities or *guna*s, the interplay of which permeates the material world
prana air	:	life-force; the breath of life
prarabdha	:	the deeds of one's past birth
purusasukta	:	hymns of *Rigveda*
Rahu	:	the eighth planet of Hindu astrology; an evil omen
rechaka	:	exhalation through the right nostril in *pranayama*
Rohini	:	the forth asterism in a constellation of five stars; the daughter of Daksha and wife of Chandra.
Rudra	:	Lord Shiva in His most terrible form
Rukmini	:	Daughter of Bhismaka, king of Bidarva and Krisha's chief queen.

Rukmini's consort	:	Krishna
rudraksha	:	a big wild tree, the seeds of which are made into a rosary, held most sacred and mostly used by ascetics.
salagram	:	a perforated geode stone collected from the Gandaki River and worshipped as Vishnu.
samadhi	:	The highest goal of a *yogi* is to reach this unitive state in which the meditator becomes enmeshed with the object or focus of his meditation.
Samkhya	:	a system of philosophy invented by Kapila (600 BCE) based on the duality of *prakriti* and *purusa*
sannyasi	:	a monk who has renounced all worldly things
Sarada	:	Sarasvati; Goddes of Learning
sattva, rajas, tamas	:	represent creation, preservation and destruction
seven vital constituents	:	bone, marrow, flesh, glands, blood, skin and semen
shakti	:	energy
Shuka	:	son of Vyasa who read out the *Bhagavata* to the dying King Parikshit
Shukra	:	Shukracharya, the son of Sage Bhrigu and *guru* of the demons
siddhi	:	enlightenment
six branches of the Vedas	:	Siksha, Kalpa, Vyakarana, Nirukta, Jyotisa and Chhanda
six enemies	:	six passions such as lust, anger, greed, attachment, inebriation and immoral relationship
six-petalled lotus	:	*Svadhisthana chakra*
six scriptures	:	Mimamsa (Jaimini), Vedanta (Vyasa), Uttara Mimamsa (Vyasa), Nyaya (Gautama), Samkhya (Kapila) and Patanjala (Kanada)

Sri	:	Goddess Lakshmi
Srihatta *pattana*	:	also *trikuta*; the inside middle of the forehead between the two eyebrows
Sri Purusoattama Kshetra	:	Puri, the abode of Lord Jagannatha
Sudhanidhi	:	the treasure of nectar
Surabhi	:	the cow-Goddess
sushumna	:	a *nadi* that connects *muladhara chakra* with *sahasrara*; path for the ascent of *kundalini* energy from the base of the spine to the crown of the head, the crevice of *Brahman*; the central channel for the flow of *prana* throughout the body
tailokya	:	the three worlds: heaven, the earth, and the nether world
tandava	:	a terrible dance form performed by Shiva (Nataraja) which brings destruction
three kinds of suffering	:	caused by the gods, the world and the self
trikuta	:	also Srihatta Pattana; the inside middle of the forehead between the two brows
Triveni	:	the three *nadi*s; *inala*, *pingala* and *sushumna*
'U' kara	:	in the shape of the Odia alphabet 'U'
ulluka vidya	:	the art of making oneself invisible or taking various forms
Uma	:	name of Parvati in her previous birth
Vaivasvata	:	also Vivasvata Manu; the progenitor of mankind
Vasudeva	:	Krishna
Vidyadhari	:	demi-Goddess
yaksha	:	custodian of the wealth of the dead
yajna	:	ceremonial holy fire
Yajnavalkya	:	a sage; author of *Shukla Yajurveda*
yojana	:	eight miles approximately